MW01644986

This book belongs to:

....

E-mail: ....

Adress: ....

Phone: ....

Take Care

OF THE PEOPLE YOU LOVE
BUT TAKE EVEN BETTER CARE
OF THE PEOPLE THAT LOVE YOU

DATE:

I allow myself to feel___about...

DATE:

I achieved these goals this year

DATE:

5 things I love about myself are...

DATE:

Before I die, I want to..

DATE:

As a child, my favorite toy was...

DATE:

As a child, my favorite subject in school was...

DATE:

As a child, most of all I loved to

DATE:

Being confident means....

Date: ______________________

I am becoming more inspired by...

Date: ______________________

I am able to let go of...

Date: ______________________

I always put of f_____because...

Date: ______________________

I always love doing

DATE: ____________________________

I always hate doing...

DATE: ____________________________

I always get pumped up when I...

DATE: ____________________________

I always feel rushed when I...

DATE: ____________________________

I always feel happy when I...

Date:

I am most energized when I...

Date:

I am most anxious about...

Date:

I am living my best life right now by...

Date:

I am intelligent because...

DATE:

I am grateful for my job because...

DATE:

I am going to try to be better at...

DATE:

I am focusing my attention on...

DATE:

I am capable of...

DATE:

I am special because...

DATE:

I am so blessed to be able to...

DATE:

I am most relaxed when I...

DATE:

I am most proud of myself for...

DATE:

I am most productive when...

DATE:

I am most inspired by...

DATE:

I am most in tune with...

DATE:

I am most happy when I am...

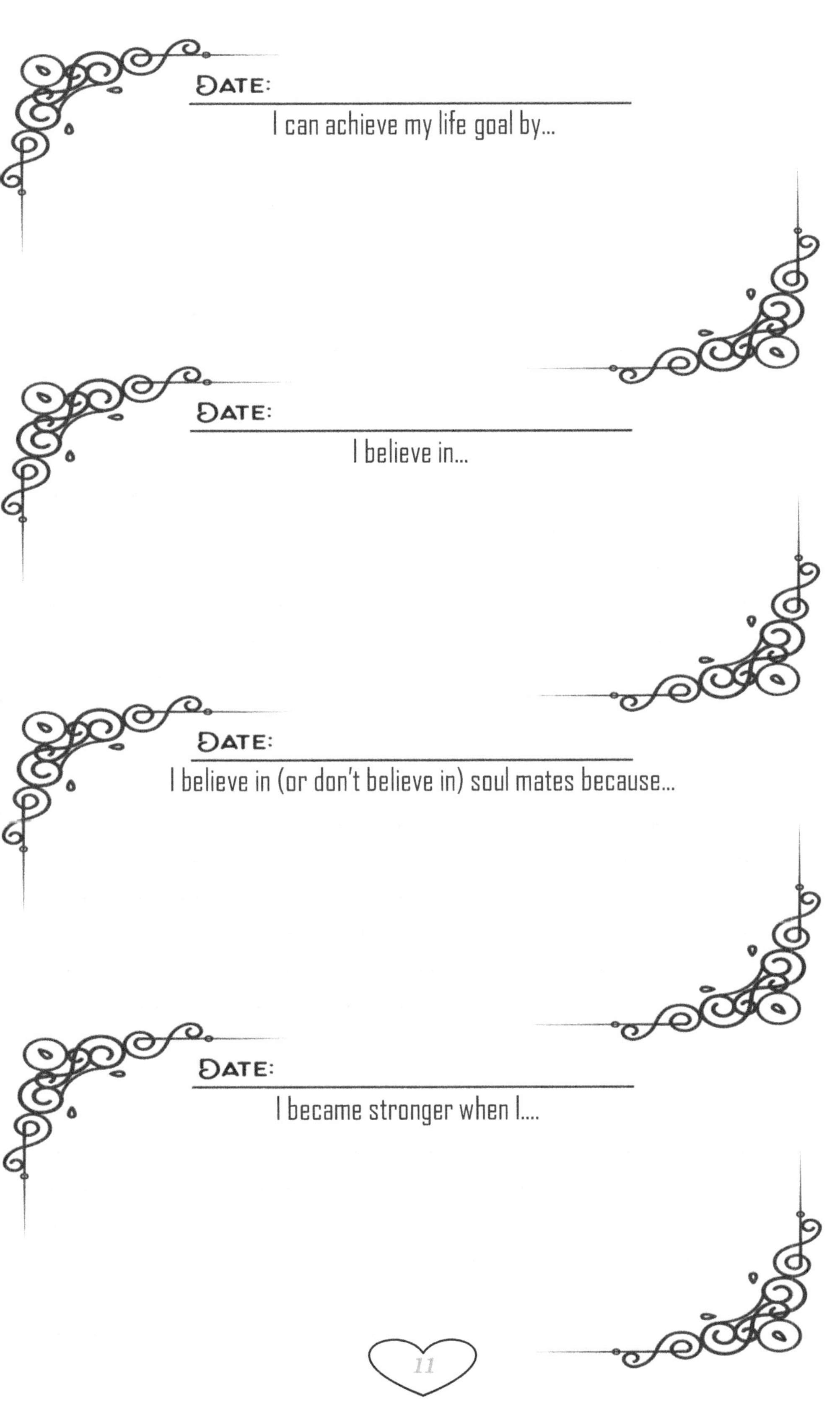

DATE:

I can achieve my life goal by...

DATE:

I believe in...

DATE:

I believe in (or don't believe in) soul mates because...

DATE:

I became stronger when I....

DATE:

I appreciate my siblings because...

DATE:

I appreciate my family because...

DATE:

I am worried about...

DATE:

I am unique because...

If You Can
Dream It,
YOU CAN
DO IT

DATE: ______

I can follow my passion by...

DATE: ______

I can enjoy nature today by...

DATE: ______

I can do better at my current job by...

DATE: ______

I can describe myself with these four words...

DATE:

I can better serve my community by...

DATE:

I can better manage my stress by...

DATE:

I can be more confident in myself by...

DATE:

I can be more childlike by...

DATE:

I can show my kids I'm proud of them by...

DATE:

I can show my kids I love them today by...

DATE:

I can practice more patience when...

DATE:

I can make tomorrow better by...

DATE:

I can make the world a better place by...

DATE:

I can make better use of my time by...

DATE:

I can inspire someone by...

DATE:

I can help someone today by...

DATE:

I can take better care of myself by...

DATE:

I can strengthen my resolve by...

DATE:

I can strengthen my faith by...

DATE:

I can spend more time with my friends by...

DATE: ____________________

I can spend more quality time with my family by...

DATE: ____________________

I can simplify my life today by...

DATE: ____________________

I can show myself love today by...

DATE: ____________________

I can show my partner I'm proud of them today by...

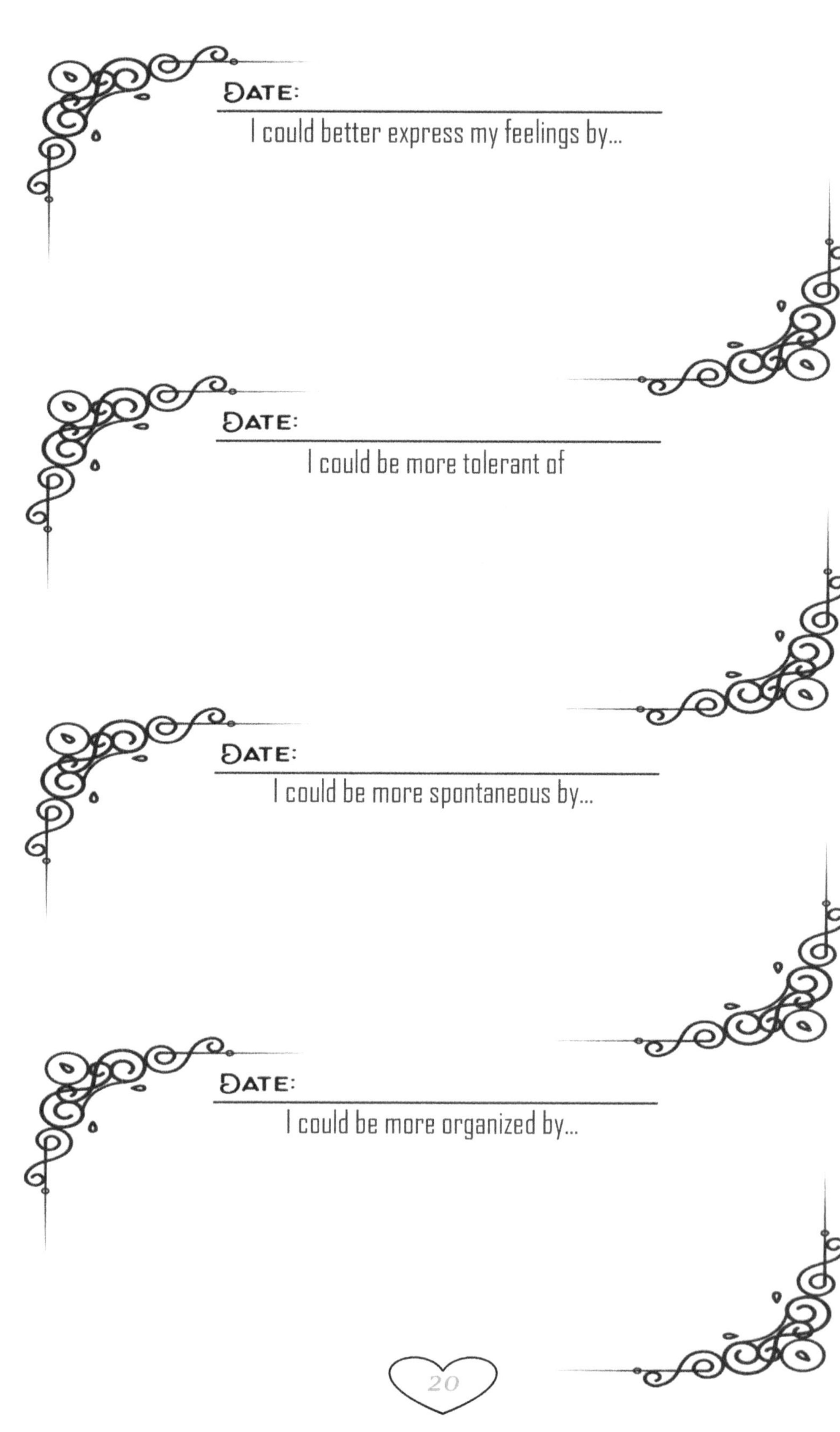

DATE:

I could better express my feelings by...

DATE:

I could be more tolerant of

DATE:

I could be more spontaneous by...

DATE:

I could be more organized by...

DATE: ____________________

I can't wait to...

DATE: ____________________

I can't go without...

DATE: ____________________

I can't go a day without...

DATE: ____________________

I can use these talents and skills to improve someone's life...

DATE:

I could put more ef fort into...

DATE:

I could open myself to new opportunities by...

DATE:

I could improve this aspect of my life...

DATE:

I could improve my mindset by...

DATE:

I could improve my biggest weakness by...

DATE:

I could get rid of this unhealthy habit...

DATE:

I could earn more money by...

DATE:

I could donate money to...

DATE:

I feel I'm at my best when...

DATE:

I envy _____ because...

DATE:

I feel fulfilled in my career by...

DATE:

I envy _____ because...

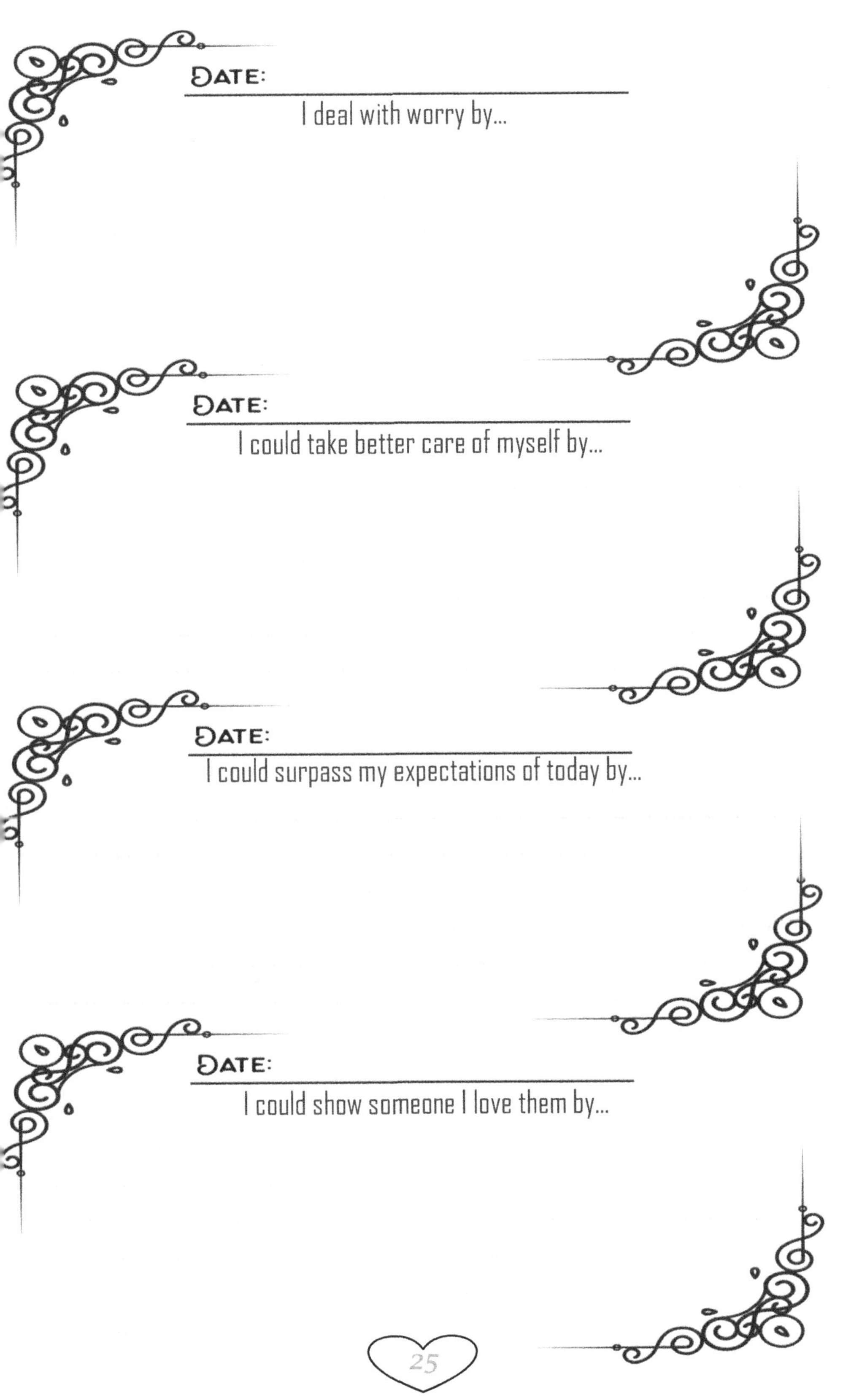

DATE:

I deal with worry by...

DATE:

I could take better care of myself by...

DATE:

I could surpass my expectations of today by...

DATE:

I could show someone I love them by...

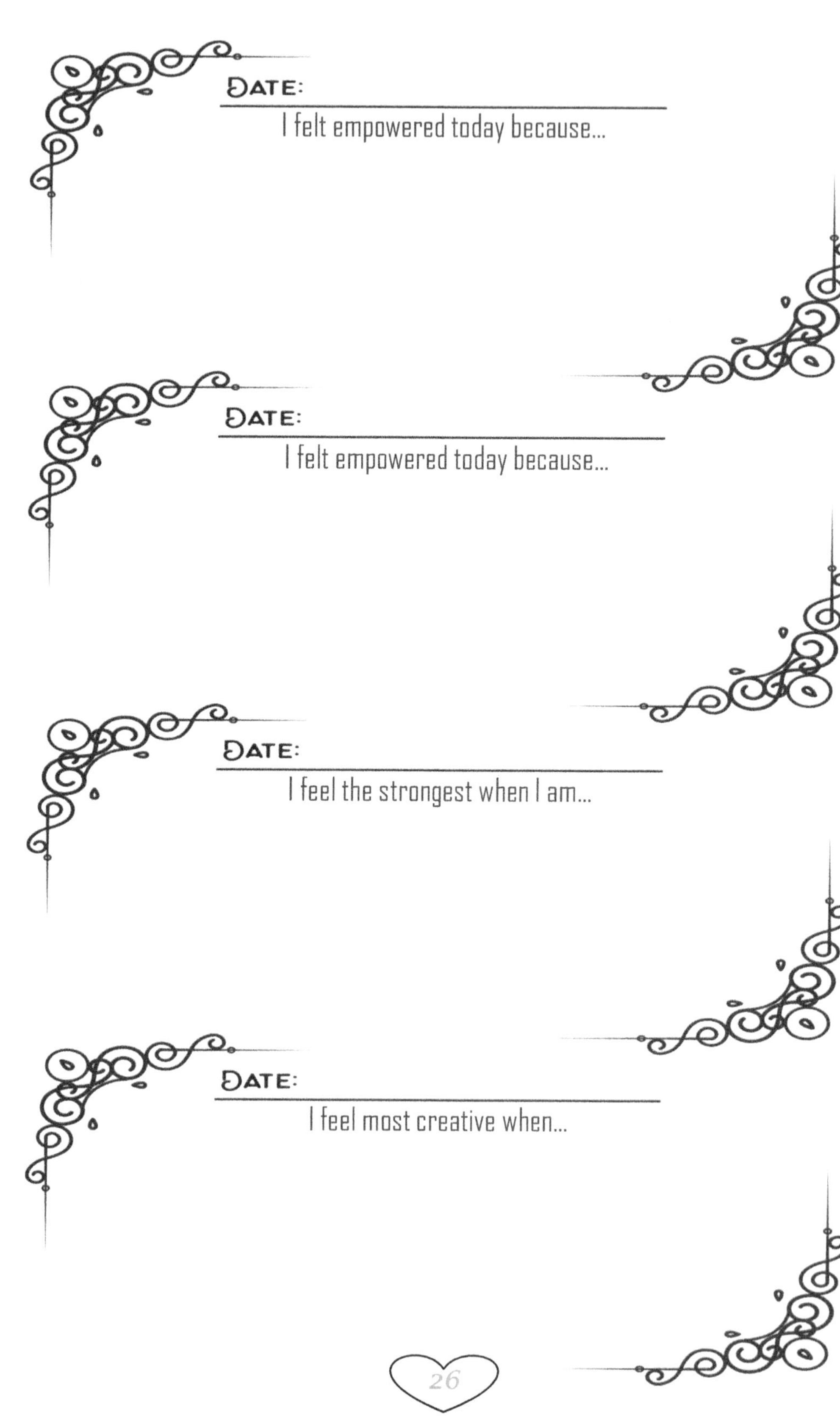

DATE:

I felt empowered today because...

DATE:

I felt empowered today because...

DATE:

I feel the strongest when I am...

DATE:

I feel most creative when...

Date:

I feel most confident when I'm with...

Date:

I feel most alive when I...

Date:

I feel lost when...

Date:

I feel joy when I...

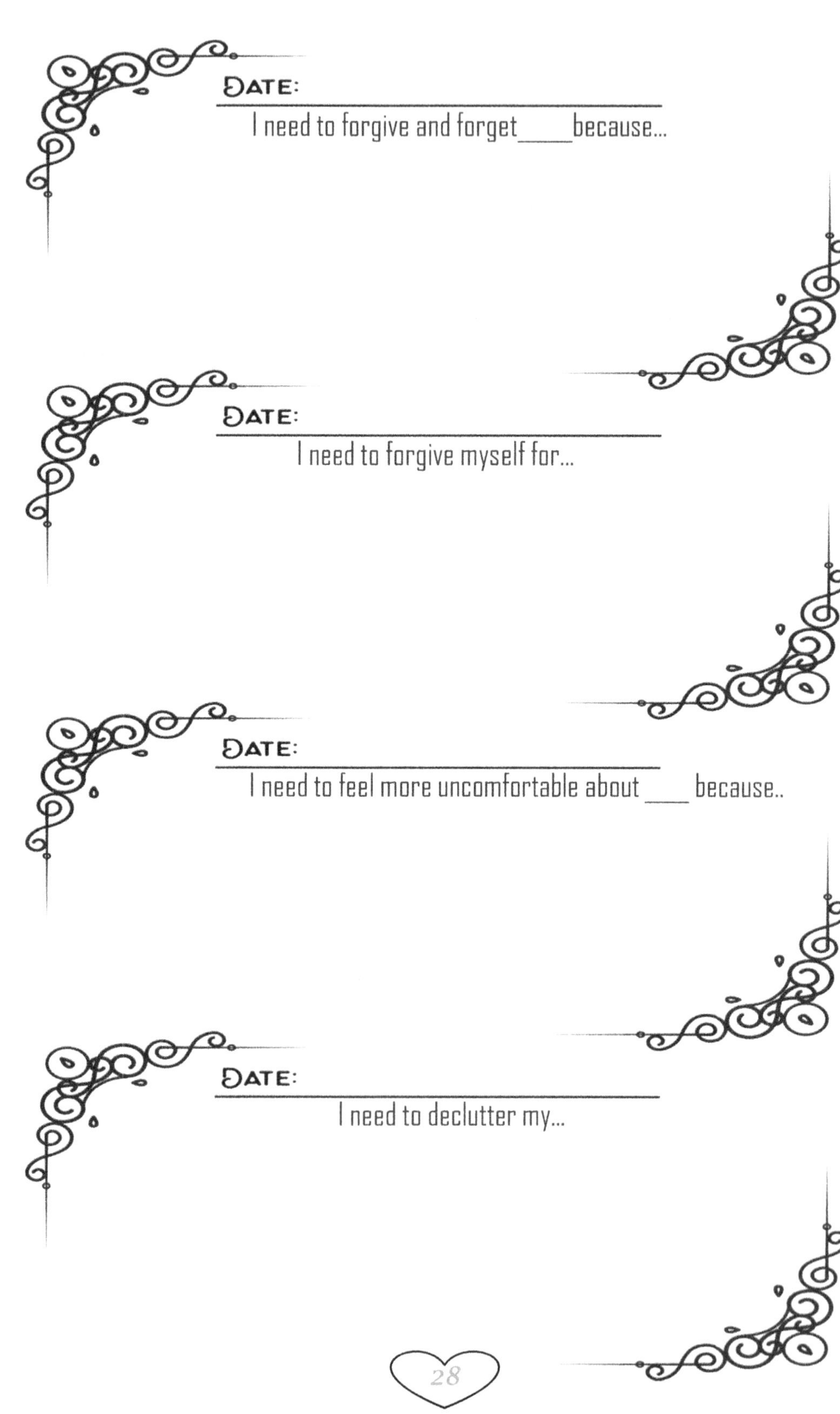

DATE: ______________________

I need to forgive and forget____because...

DATE: ______________________

I need to forgive myself for...

DATE: ______________________

I need to feel more uncomfortable about ____ because..

DATE: ______________________

I need to declutter my...

DATE:

I need to consider this opportunity for...

DATE:

I need to be truthful with myself about...

DATE:

I need my best friend to know...

DATE:

I moved closer to my goals today by...

Create
A VISION FOR YOUR LIFE

And Let Nothing
Stop You
From Achieving It

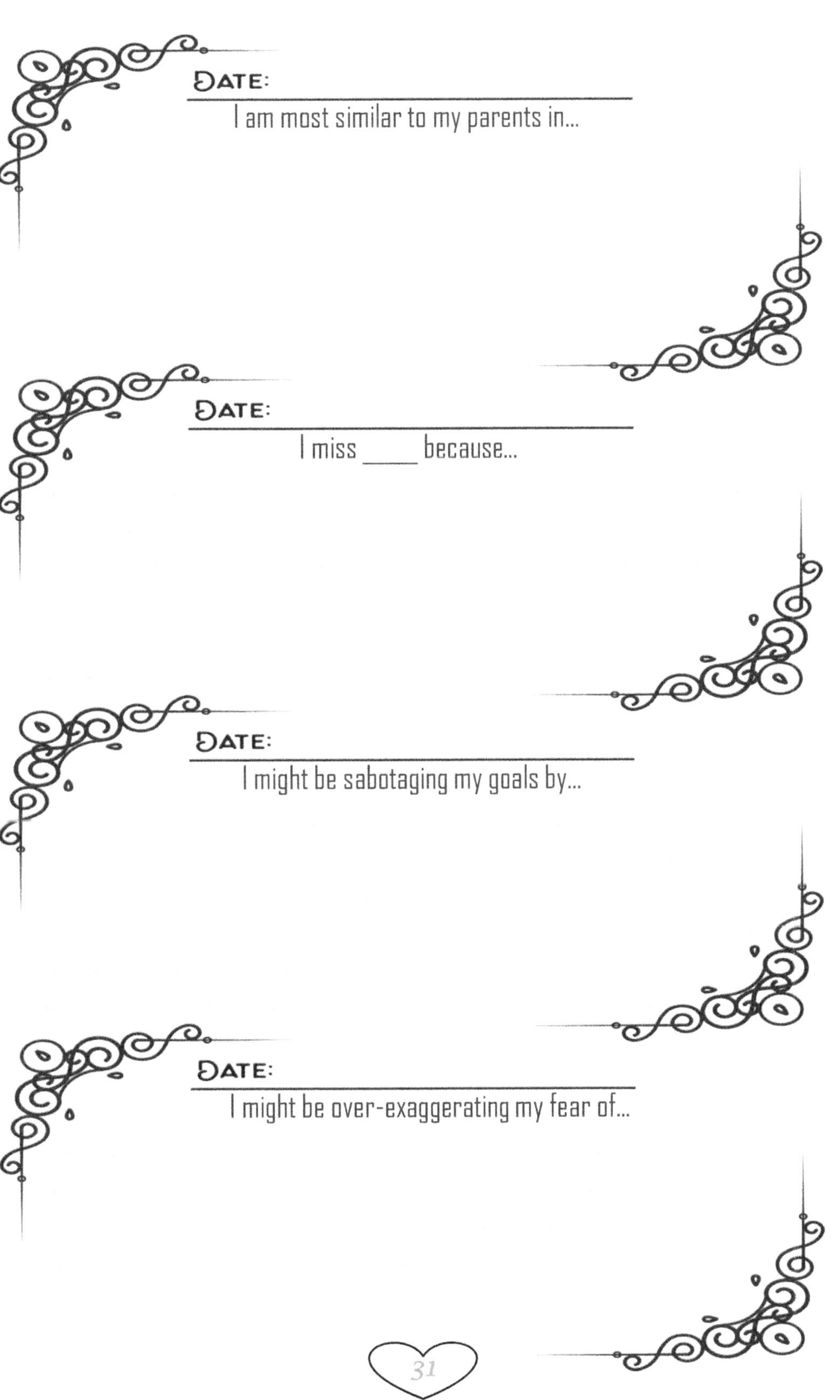

DATE:

I am most similar to my parents in...

DATE:

I miss _____ because...

DATE:

I might be sabotaging my goals by...

DATE:

I might be over-exaggerating my fear of...

DATE: ______________________

I loved doing _____ with my childhood best friend because...

DATE: ______________________

I loved doing _____ with my parents as a child because....

DATE: ______________________

I love myself because...

DATE: ______________________

I love myself because...

DATE:

I love my significant other because...

DATE:

I love my life right now because...

DATE:

I love my body because...

DATE:

I look up to...

Date:

I listened best to my intuition when I...

Date:

I know I'm successful because...

Date:

I indulge myself by...

Date:

I have changed by...

DATE:

I have been worrying too much about...

DATE:

I got through today thanks to...

DATE:

I get most anxious when I...

DATE:

I pray for...

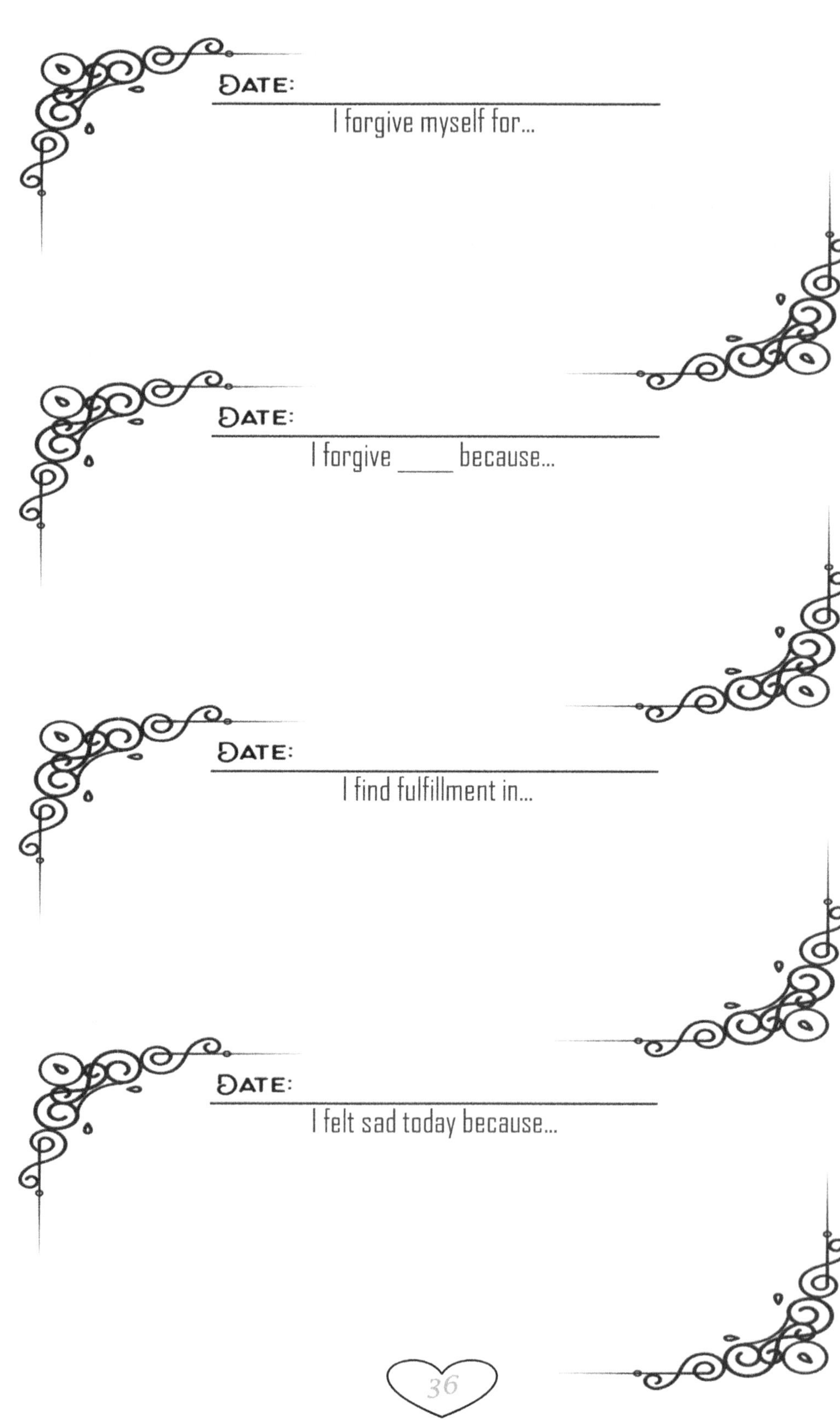

DATE:

I forgive myself for...

DATE:

I forgive _____ because...

DATE:

I find fulfillment in...

DATE:

I felt sad today because...

DATE:

I want to improve my...

DATE:

I want to be remembered for...

DATE:

I want my future self to be...

DATE:

I overvalue myself when I...

DATE:

I thought I could never....

DATE:

I stand out from the crowd because...

DATE:

I sometimes undervalue myself because...

DATE:

I smiled yesterday because...

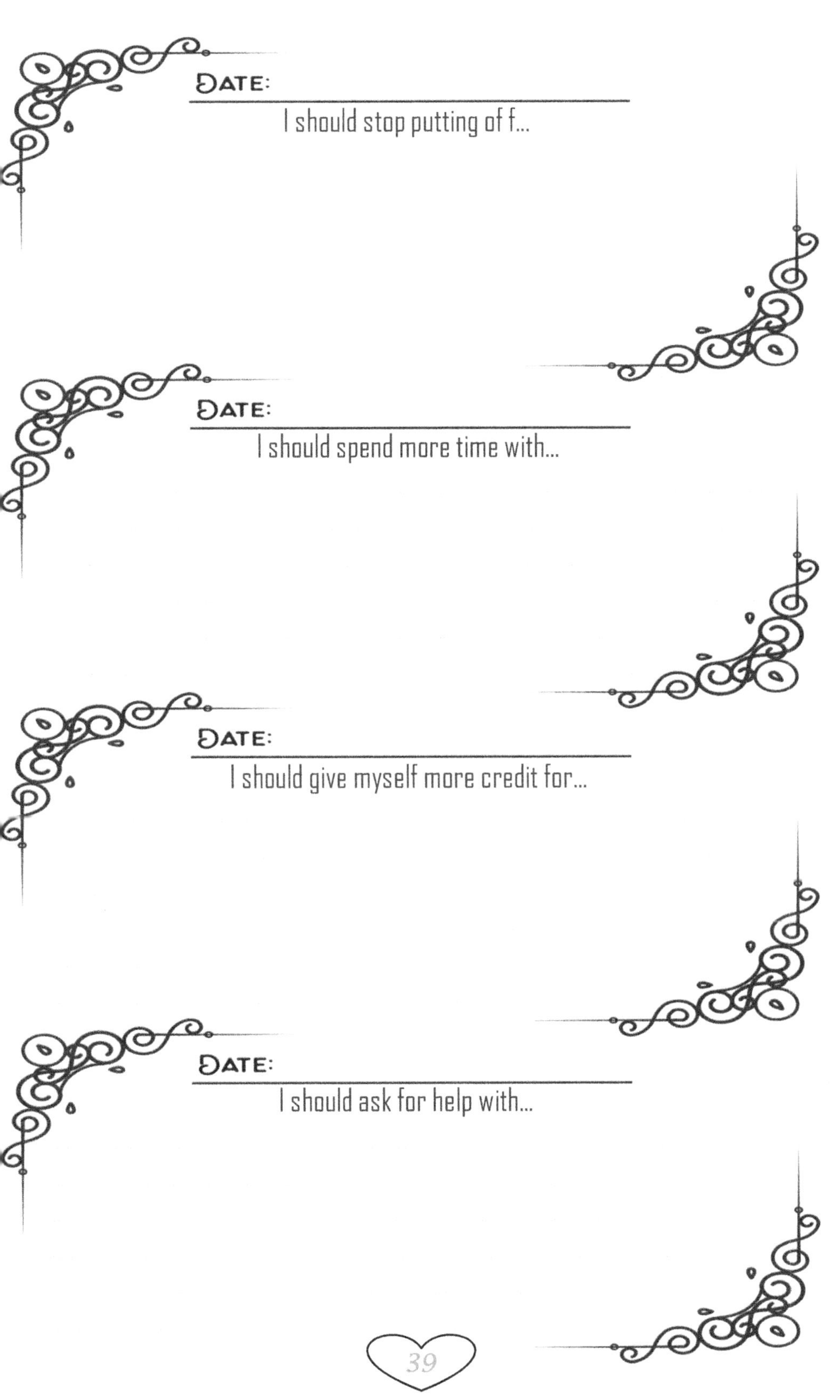

DATE:

I should stop putting off...

DATE:

I should spend more time with...

DATE:

I should give myself more credit for...

DATE:

I should ask for help with...

DATE: ______________________

I see my value in...

DATE: ______________________

I prioritize my family by...

DATE: ______________________

I no longer believe in...

DATE: ______________________

I need to say goodbye to_____because...

DATE:

I wish my spouse/significant other knew...

DATE:

I wish my children could know...

DATE:

I wish I lived in...

DATE:

I wish I knew the answer to this...

DATE:

I wish I knew more about...

DATE:

I wish I didn't have to...

DATE:

I will stop telling myself

DATE:

I will achieve my goals by...

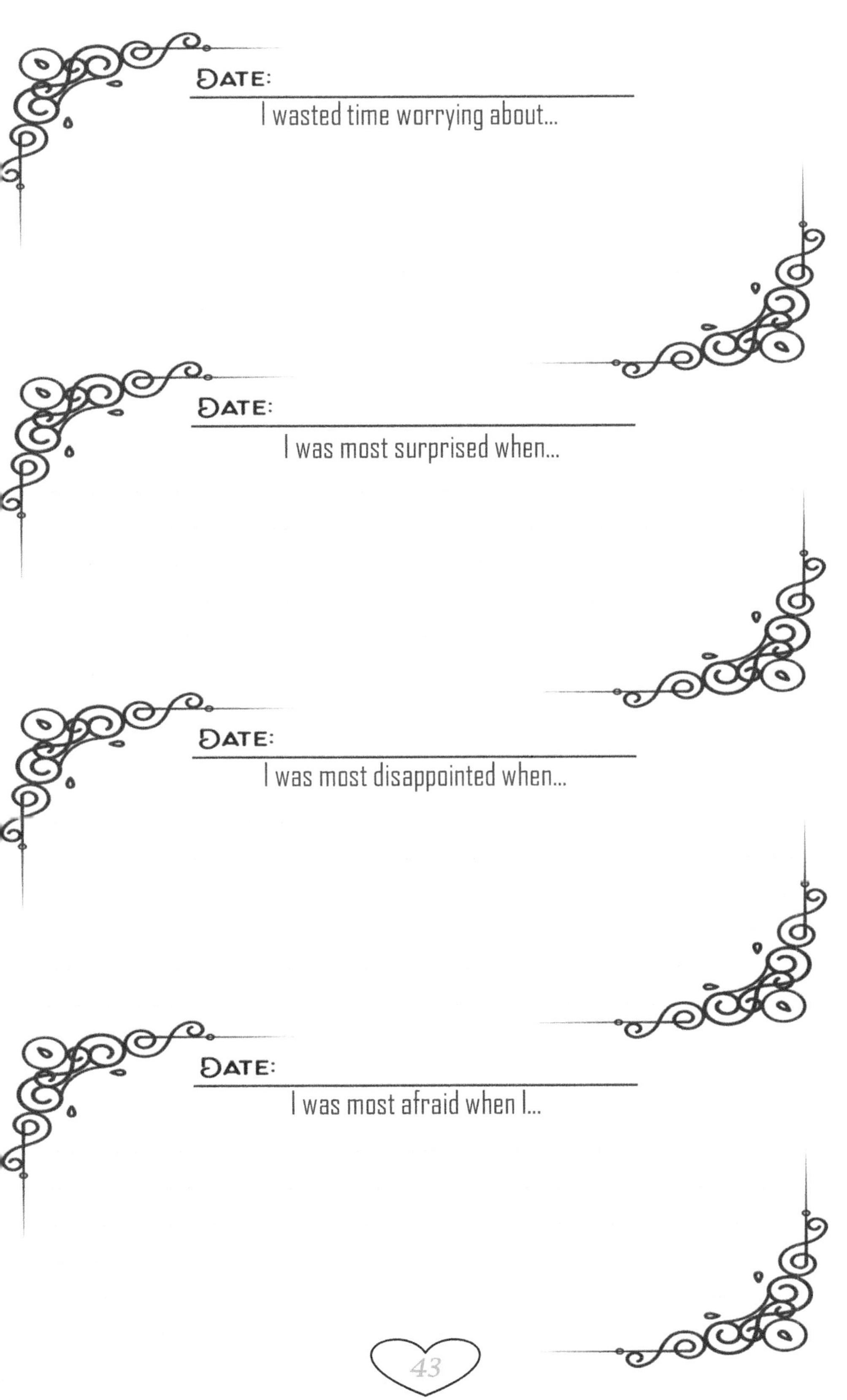

DATE:

I wasted time worrying about...

DATE:

I was most surprised when...

DATE:

I was most disappointed when...

DATE:

I was most afraid when I...

DATE: ______________________________

I was courageous this week when I...

DATE: ______________________________

I wanted to be a _____ while I was growing up because...

DATE: ______________________________

I want to read...

DATE: ______________________________

I want to learn how to

The Key
To Success
Is To Focus
On Goals
Not Obstacles

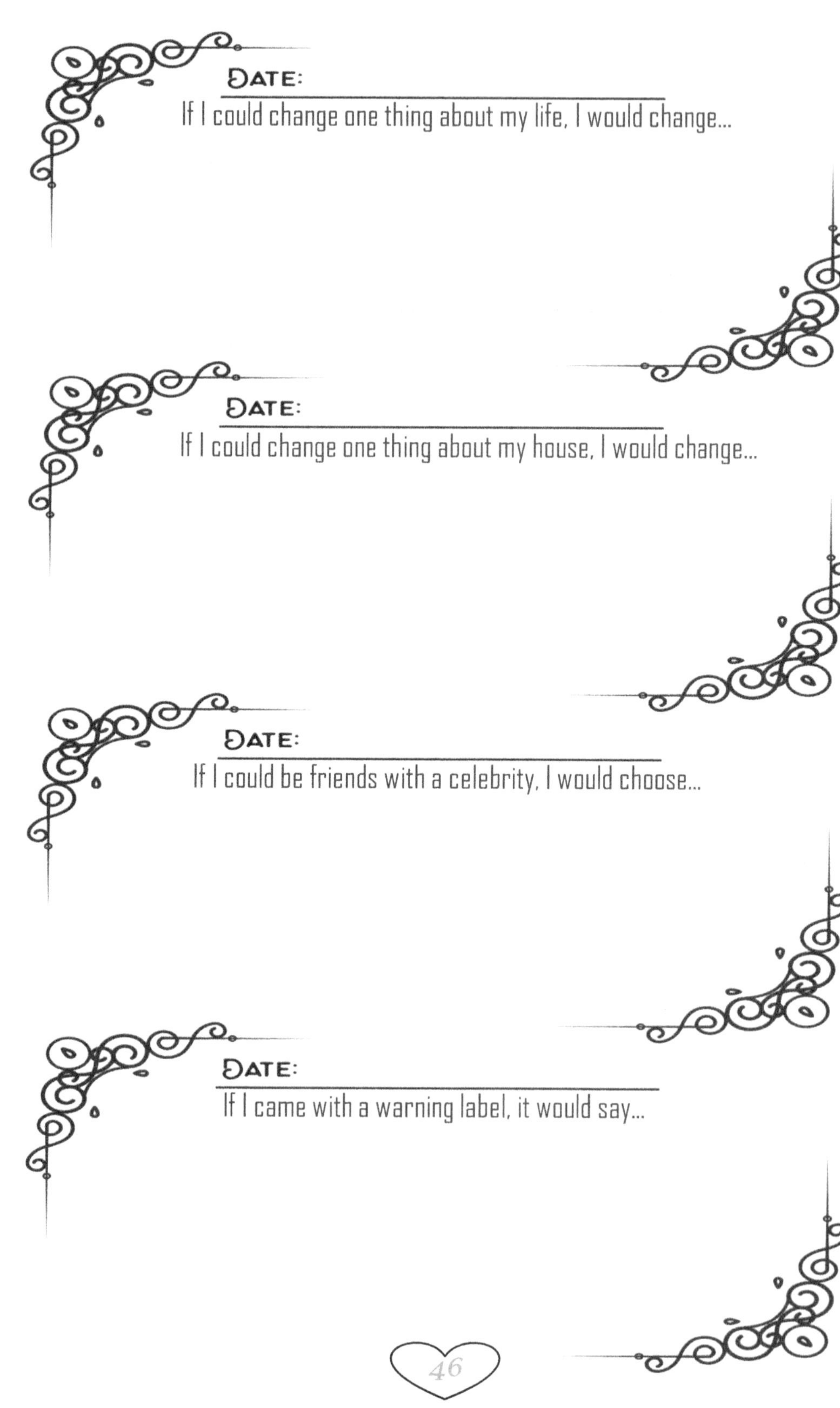

DATE:

If I could change one thing about my life, I would change...

DATE:

If I could change one thing about my house, I would change...

DATE:

If I could be friends with a celebrity, I would choose...

DATE:

If I came with a warning label, it would say...

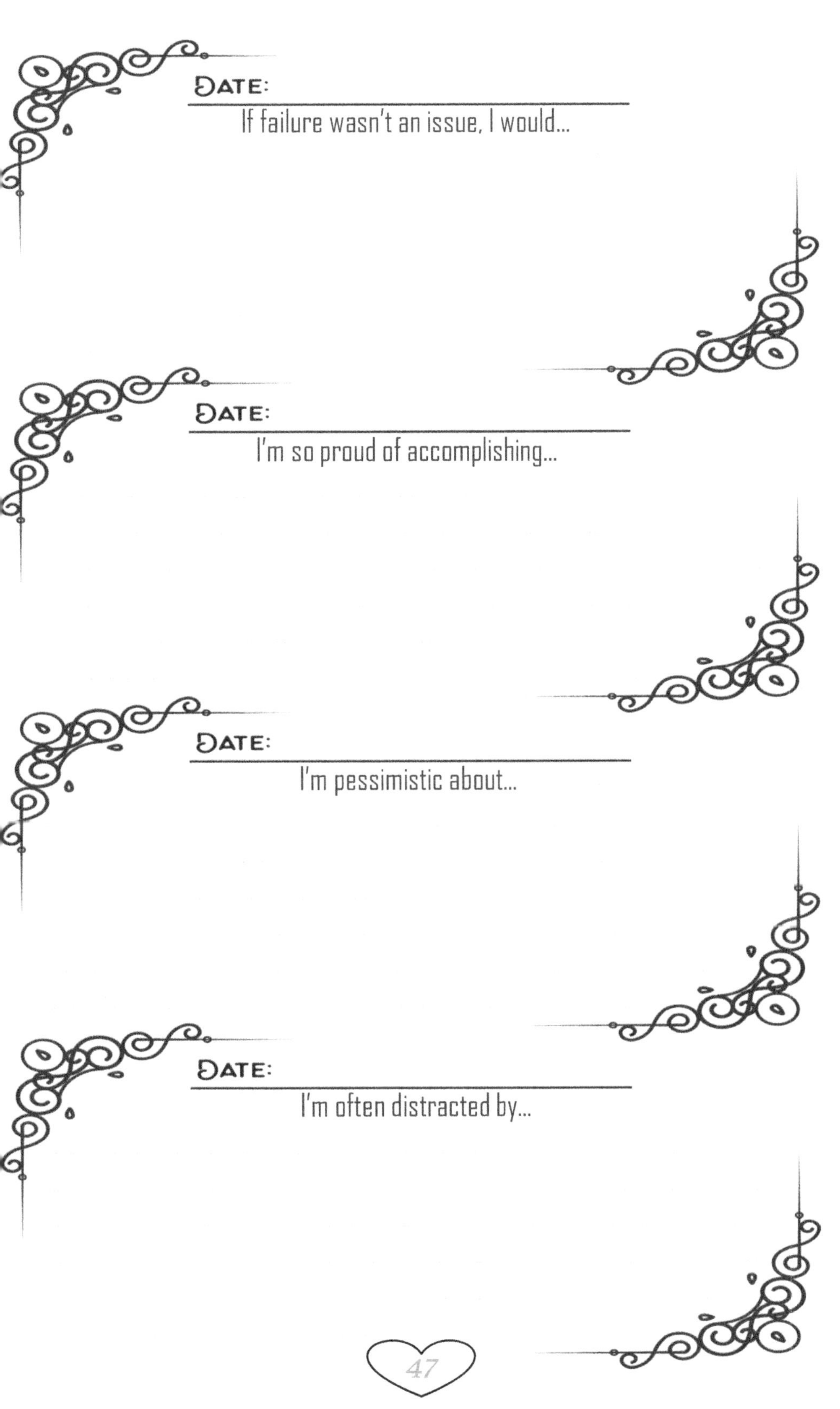

DATE:

If failure wasn't an issue, I would...

DATE:

I'm so proud of accomplishing...

DATE:

I'm pessimistic about...

DATE:

I'm often distracted by...

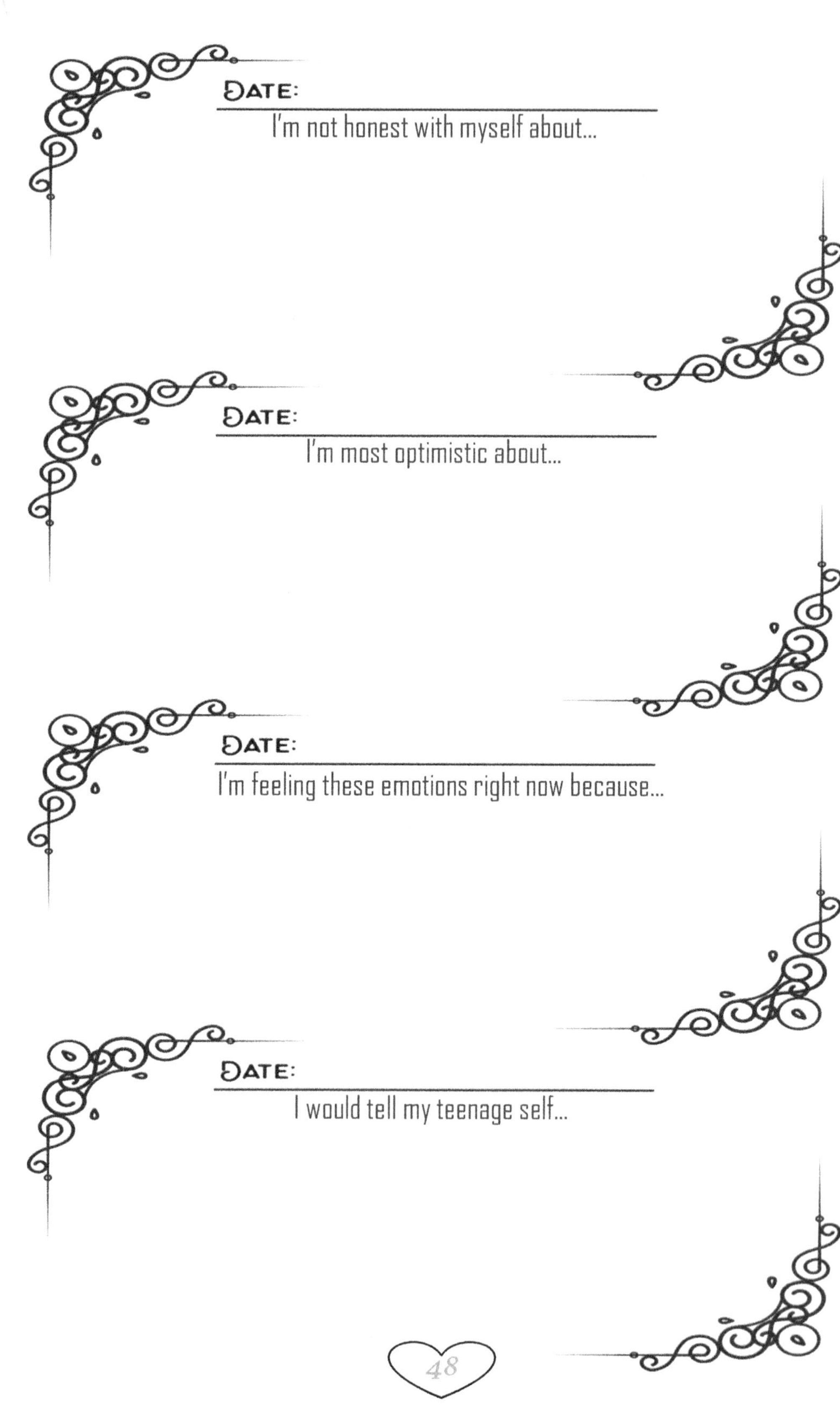

DATE:

I'm not honest with myself about...

DATE:

I'm most optimistic about...

DATE:

I'm feeling these emotions right now because...

DATE:

I would tell my teenage self...

DATE:

I would benefit from slowing down and enjoying because...

DATE:

I wish someone I love would show me by...

DATE:

I wish people saw me as...

DATE:

I wish others knew that I....

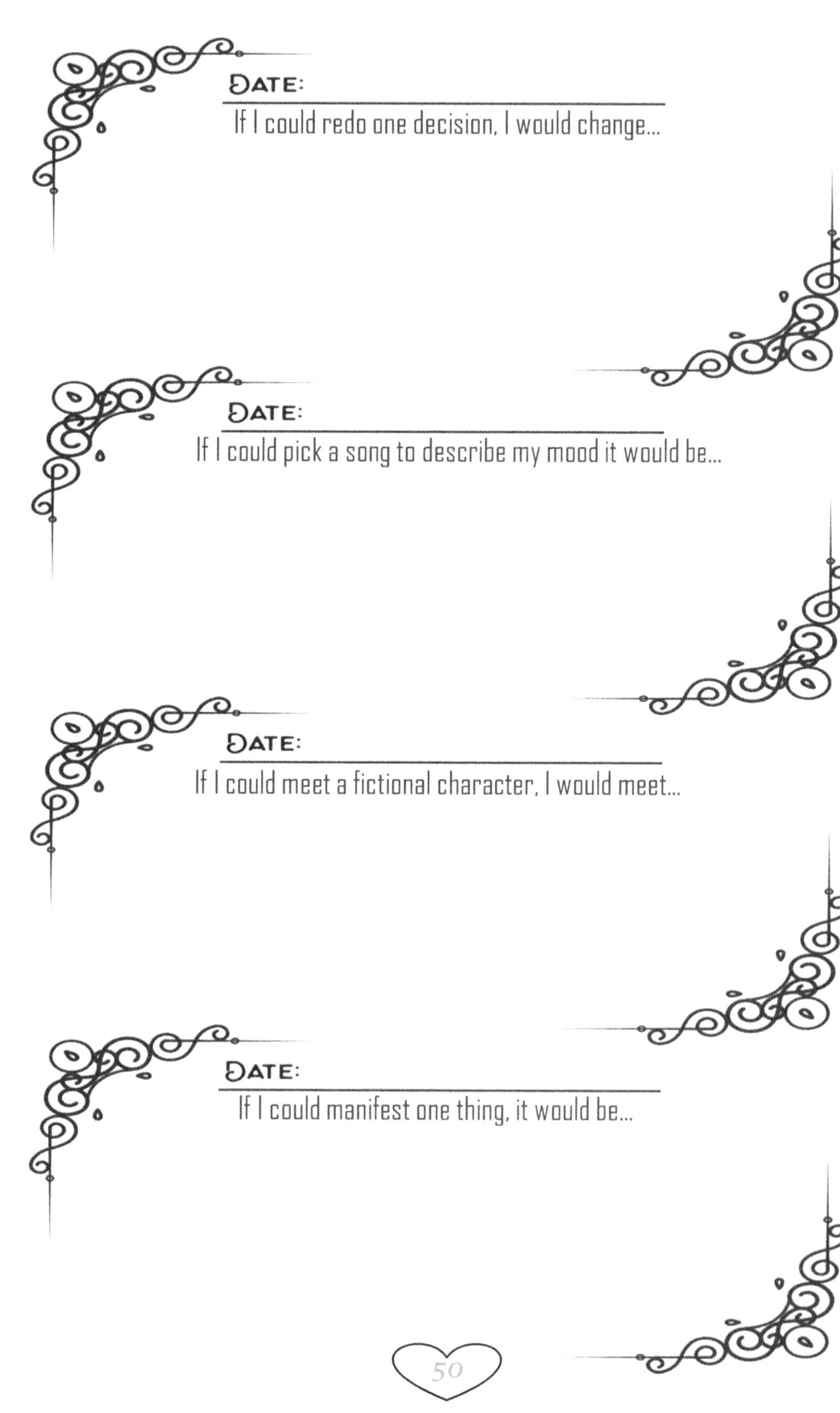

DATE:

If I could redo one decision, I would change...

DATE:

If I could pick a song to describe my mood it would be...

DATE:

If I could meet a fictional character, I would meet...

DATE:

If I could manifest one thing, it would be...

DATE:

If I could live inside one movie, I would choose...

DATE:

If I could live inside one book, I would choose...

DATE:

If I could live inside on television show, I would choose...

DATE:

If I could live in a different decade, I would live in...

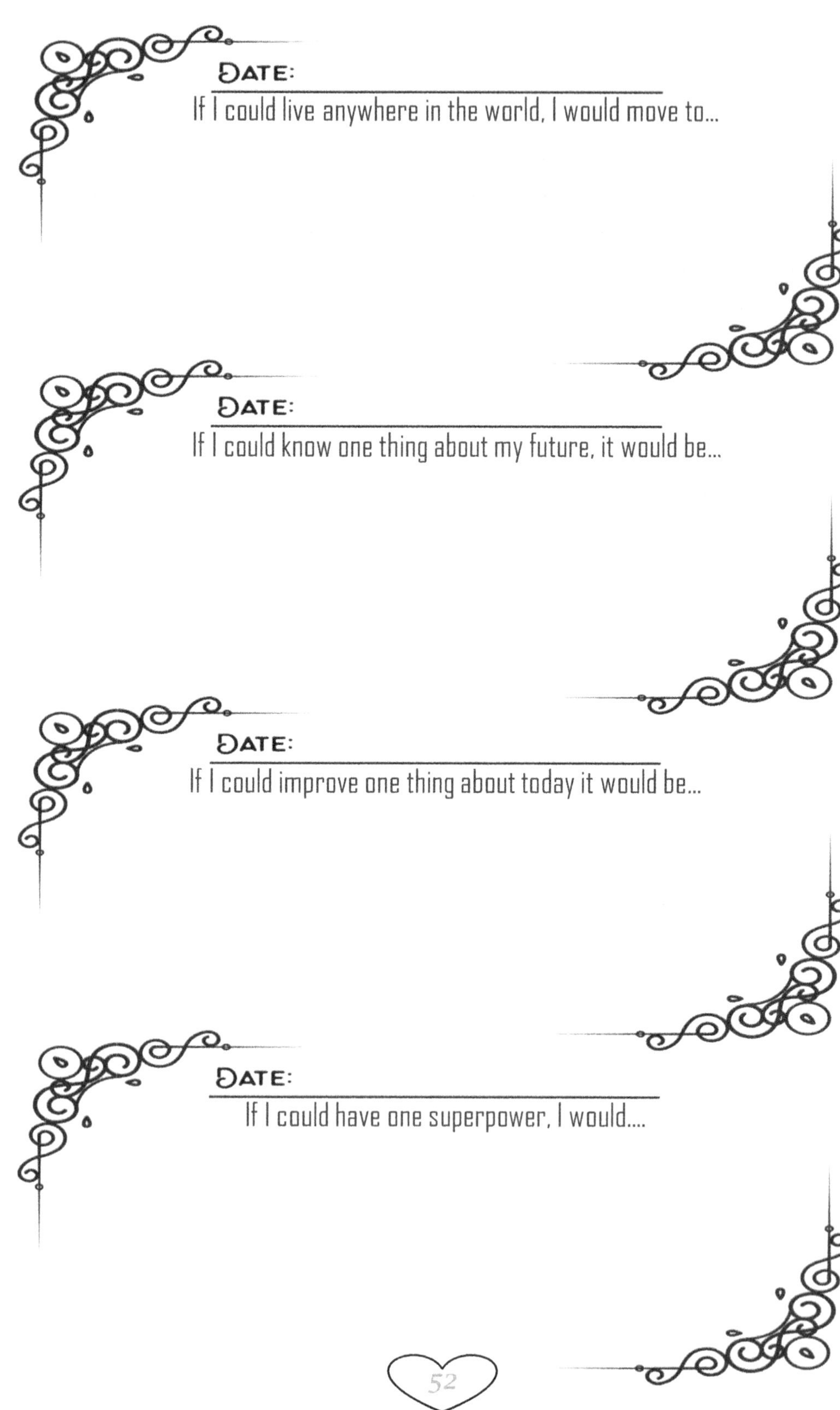

Date:

If I could live anywhere in the world, I would move to...

Date:

If I could know one thing about my future, it would be...

Date:

If I could improve one thing about today it would be...

Date:

If I could have one superpower, I would....

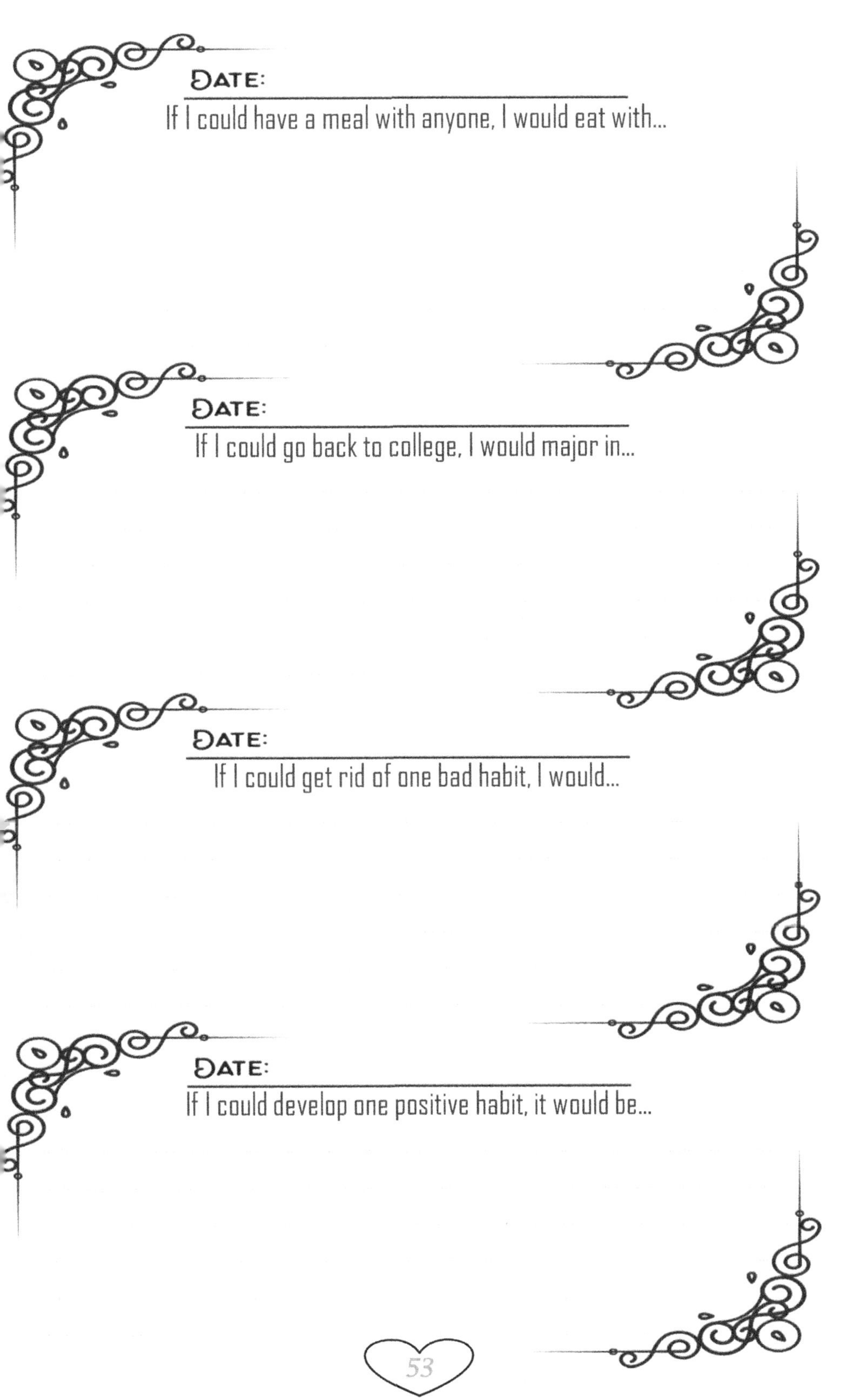

DATE:

If I could have a meal with anyone, I would eat with...

DATE:

If I could go back to college, I would major in...

DATE:

If I could get rid of one bad habit, I would...

DATE:

If I could develop one positive habit, it would be...

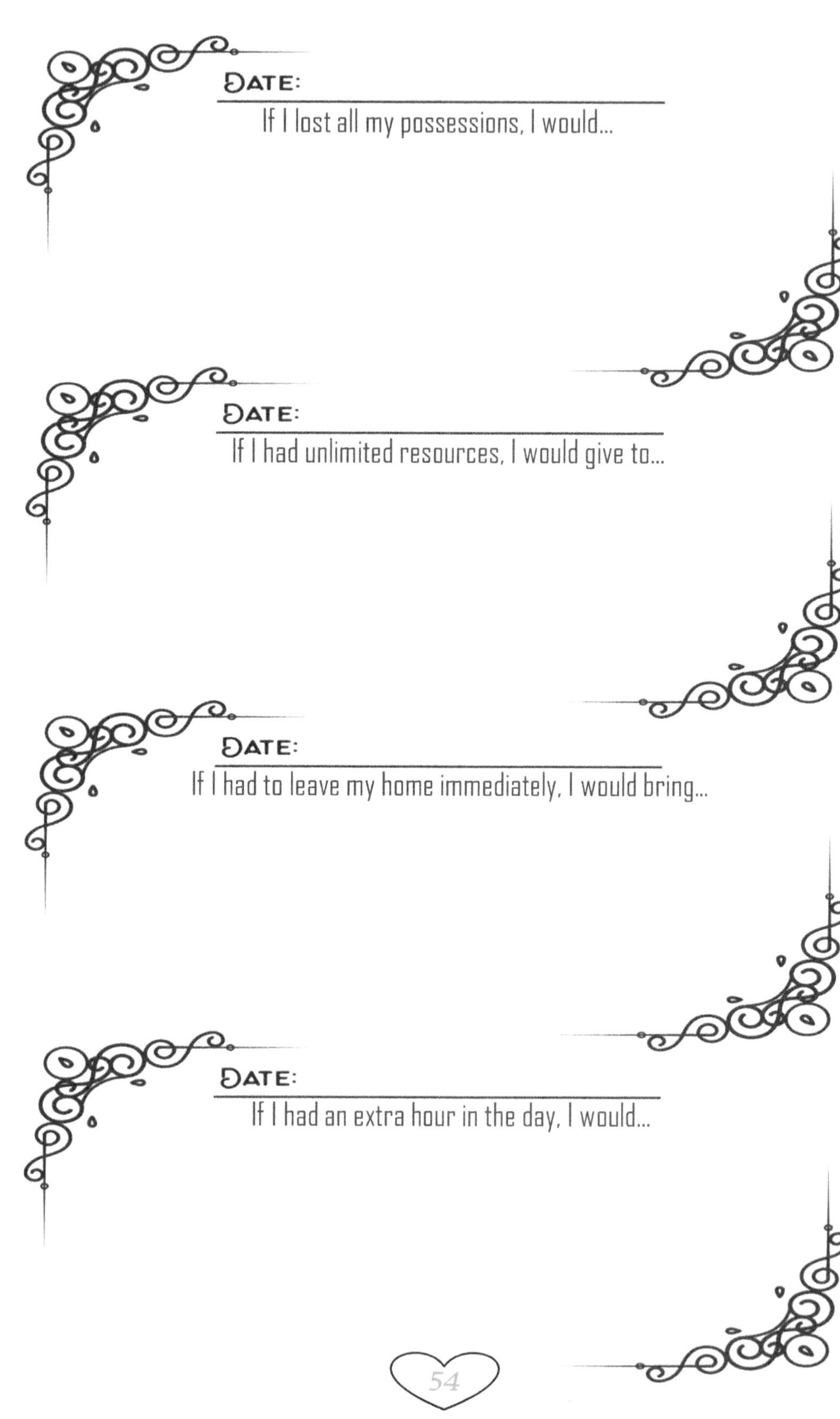

DATE:

If I lost all my possessions, I would...

DATE:

If I had unlimited resources, I would give to...

DATE:

If I had to leave my home immediately, I would bring...

DATE:

If I had an extra hour in the day, I would...

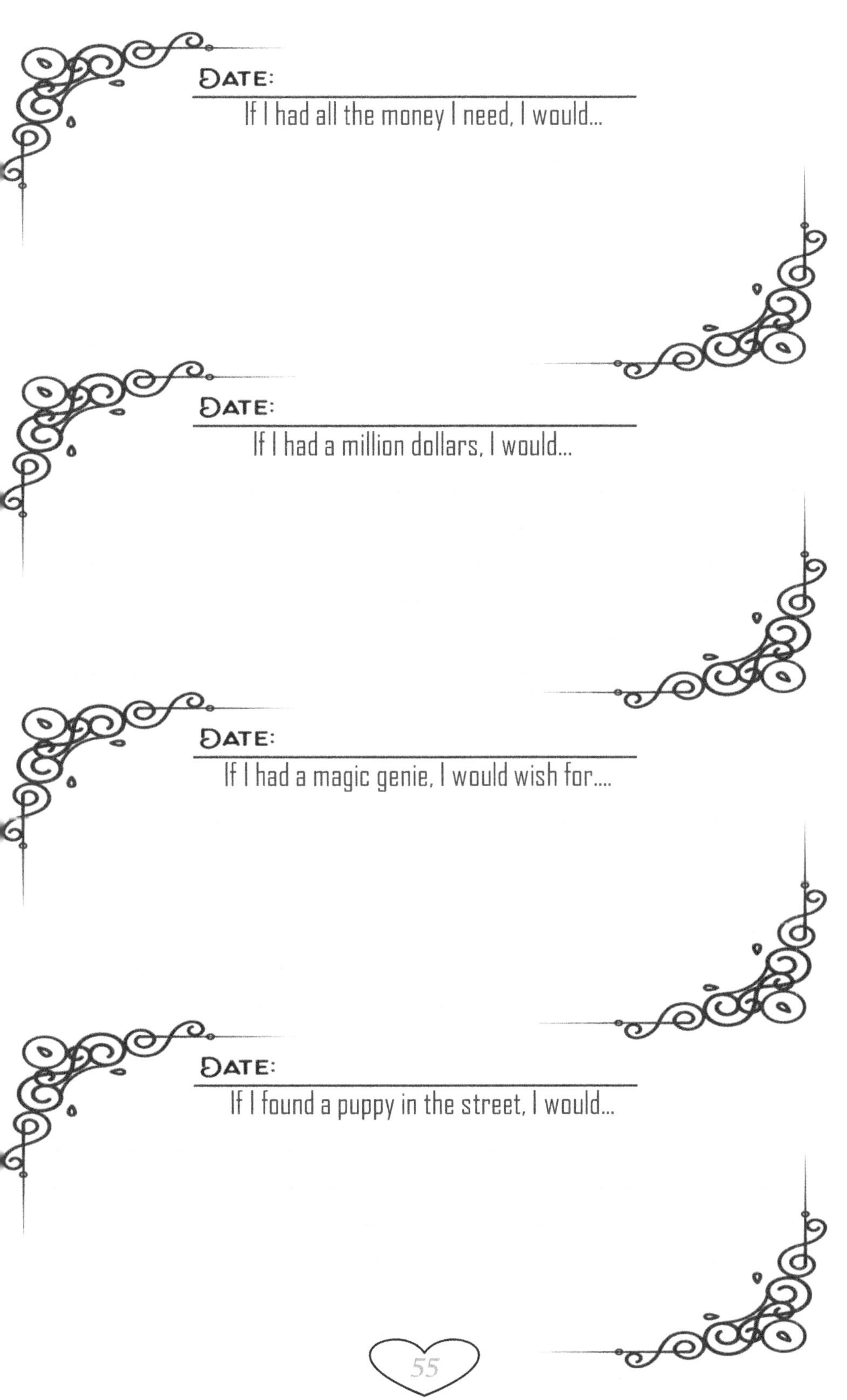

Date:

If I had all the money I need, I would...

Date:

If I had a million dollars, I would...

Date:

If I had a magic genie, I would wish for....

Date:

If I found a puppy in the street, I would...

Date:

If I could write a letter to my younger self, I would say...

Date:

If I could thank one person who inspired me, I would tell them...

Date:

If I could tell my parents one thing, I would say...

Date:

If I could start a new job, I would...

I'm Ready
FOR THE
BEST
CHAPTER
OF MY LIFE

DATE:

If I could start a new hobby, I would learn to...

DATE:

If I could speak with one person who I've lost, I would tell them...

DATE:

If I could rewrite a conversation from today, I would change...

DATE:

If I could relive one day in my life, I would redo...

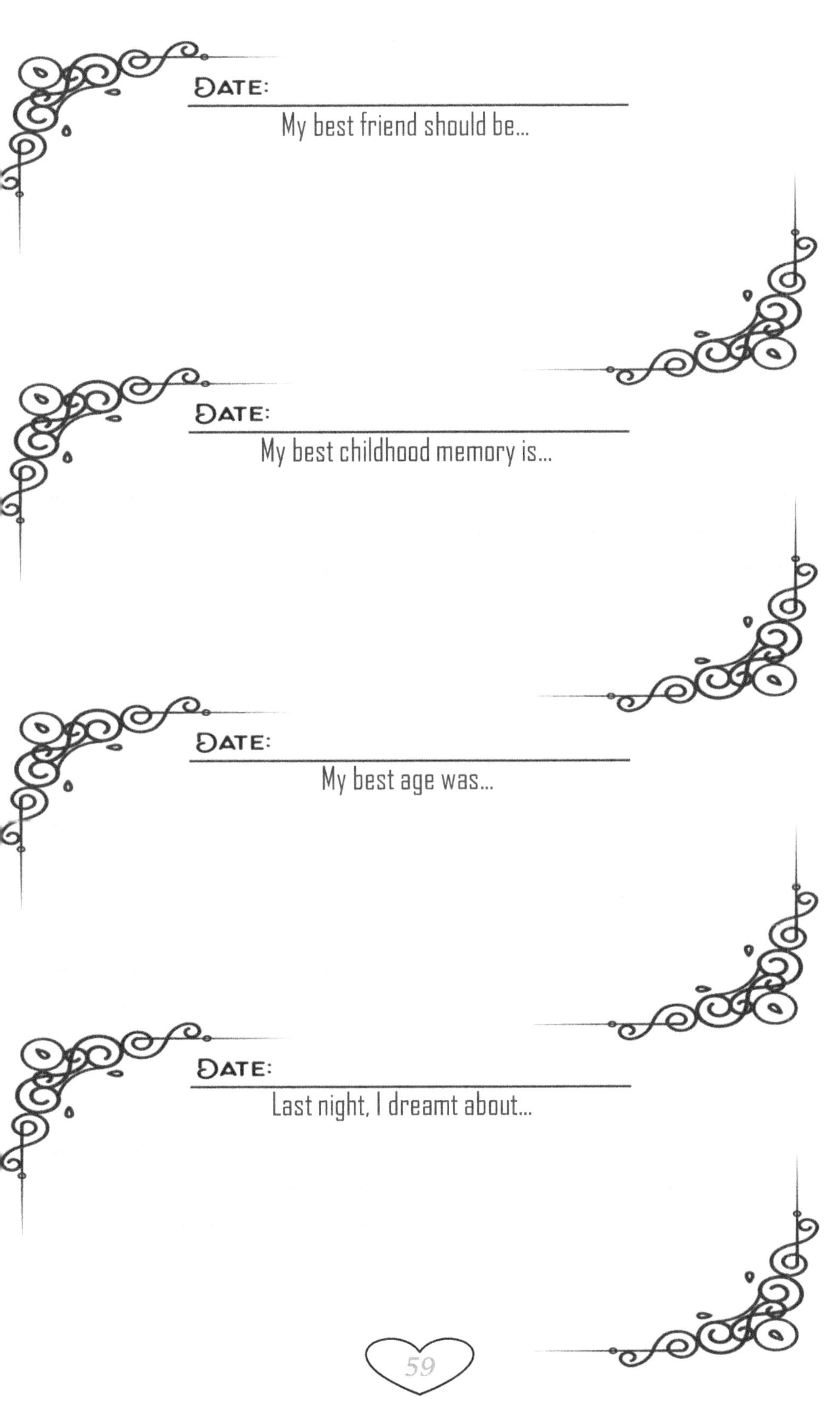

Date:

My best friend should be...

Date:

My best childhood memory is...

Date:

My best age was...

Date:

Last night, I dreamt about...

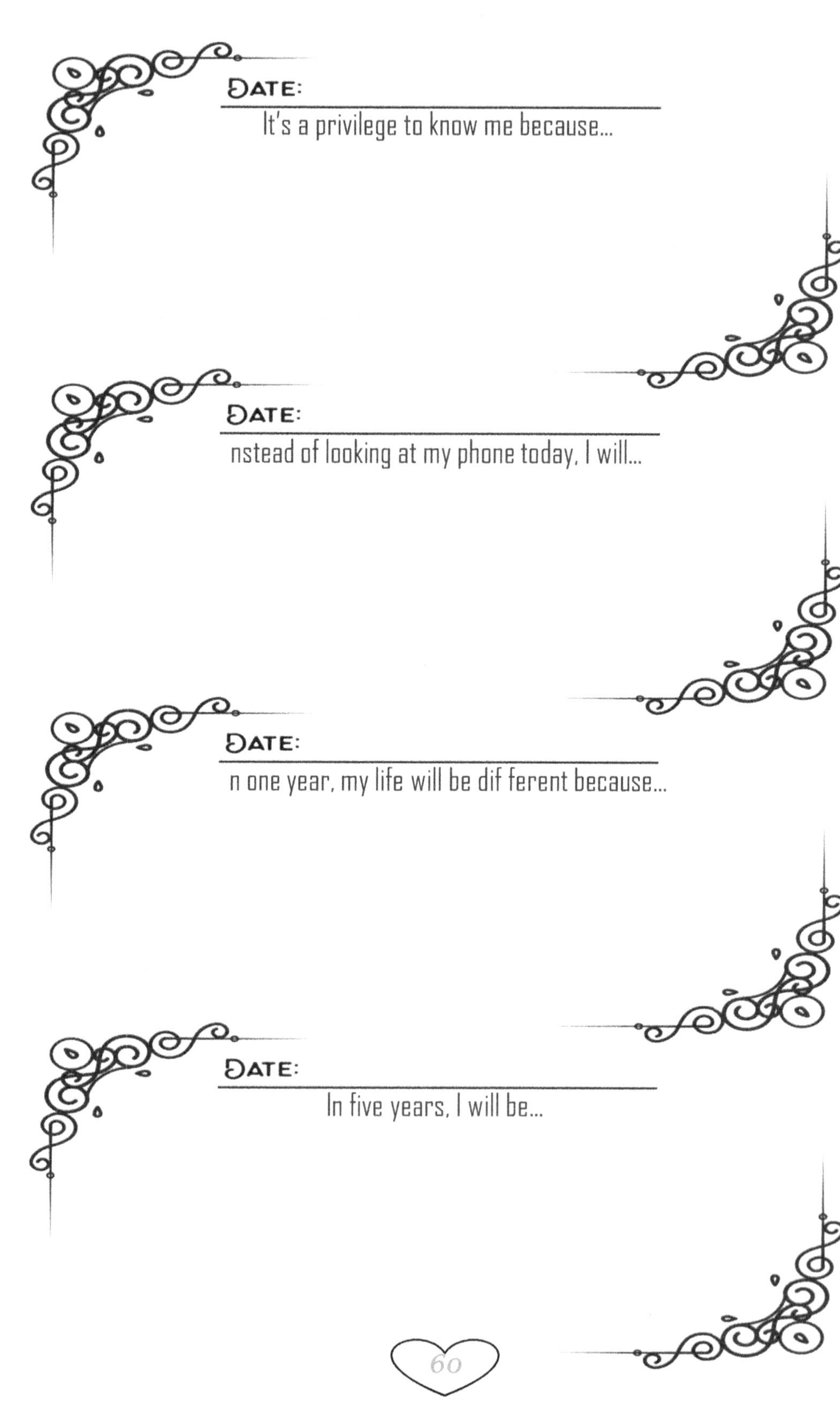

DATE:

It's a privilege to know me because...

DATE:

nstead of looking at my phone today, I will...

DATE:

n one year, my life will be dif ferent because...

DATE:

In five years, I will be...

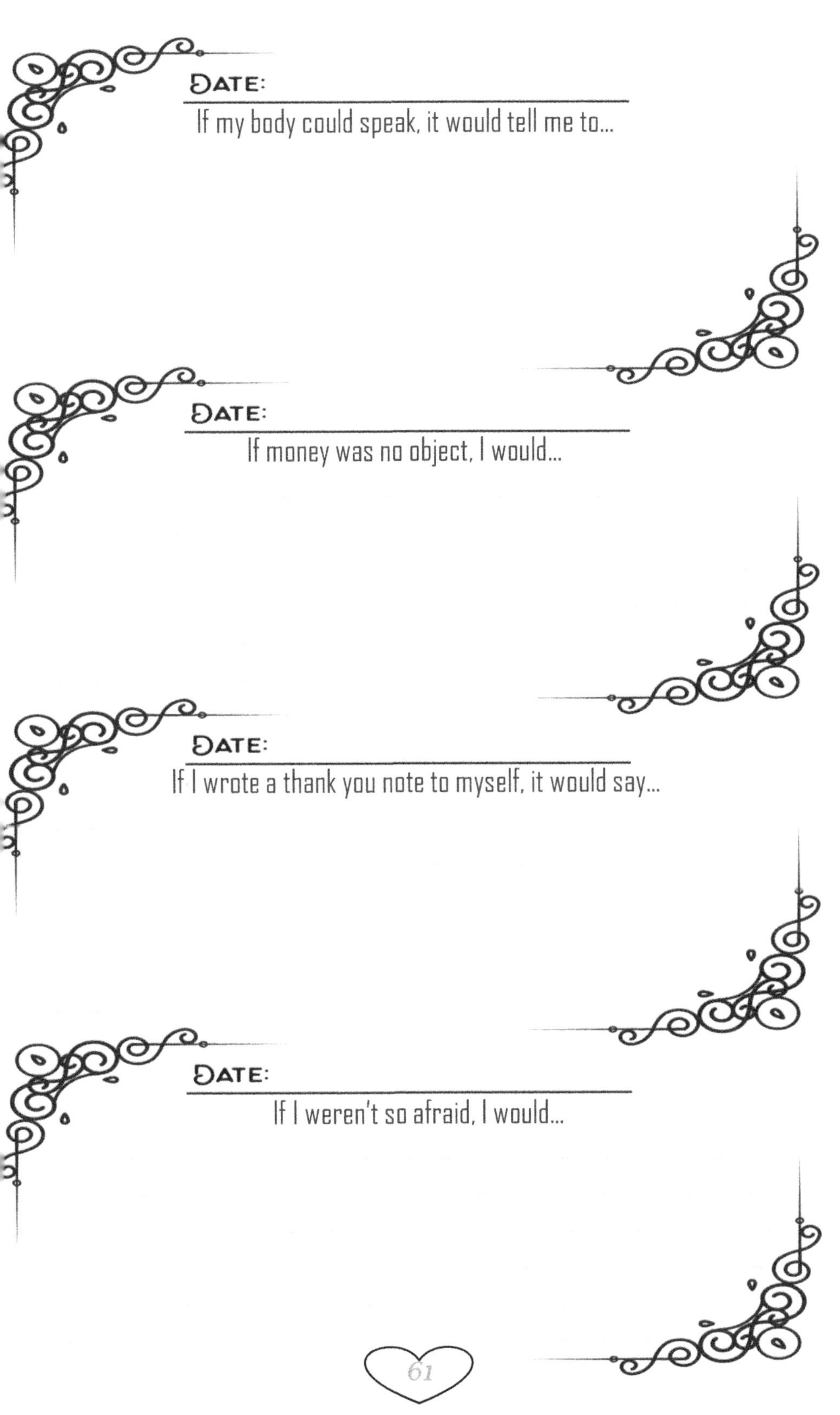

Date:

If my body could speak, it would tell me to...

Date:

If money was no object, I would...

Date:

If I wrote a thank you note to myself, it would say...

Date:

If I weren't so afraid, I would...

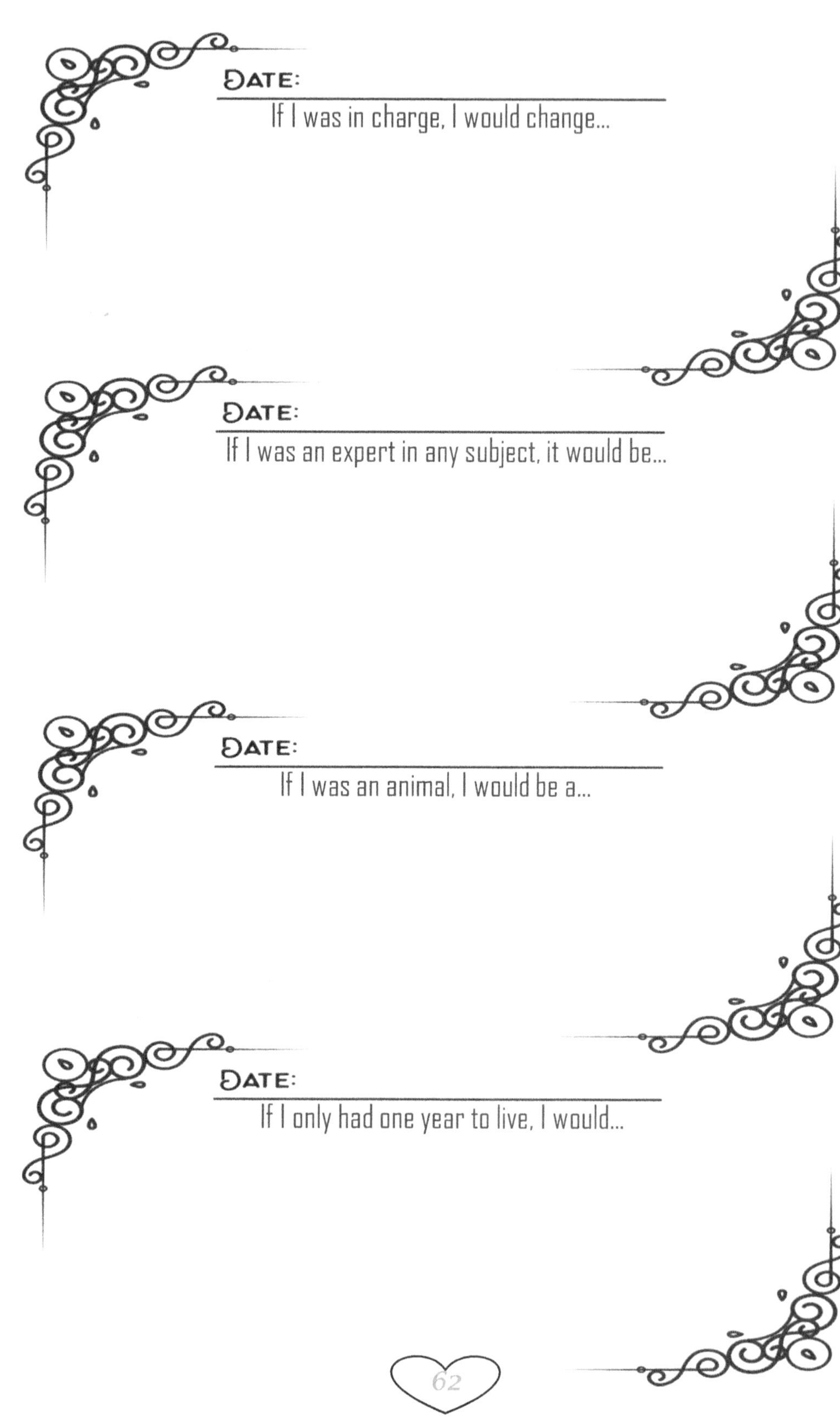

DATE:

If I was in charge, I would change...

DATE:

If I was an expert in any subject, it would be...

DATE:

If I was an animal, I would be a...

DATE:

If I only had one year to live, I would...

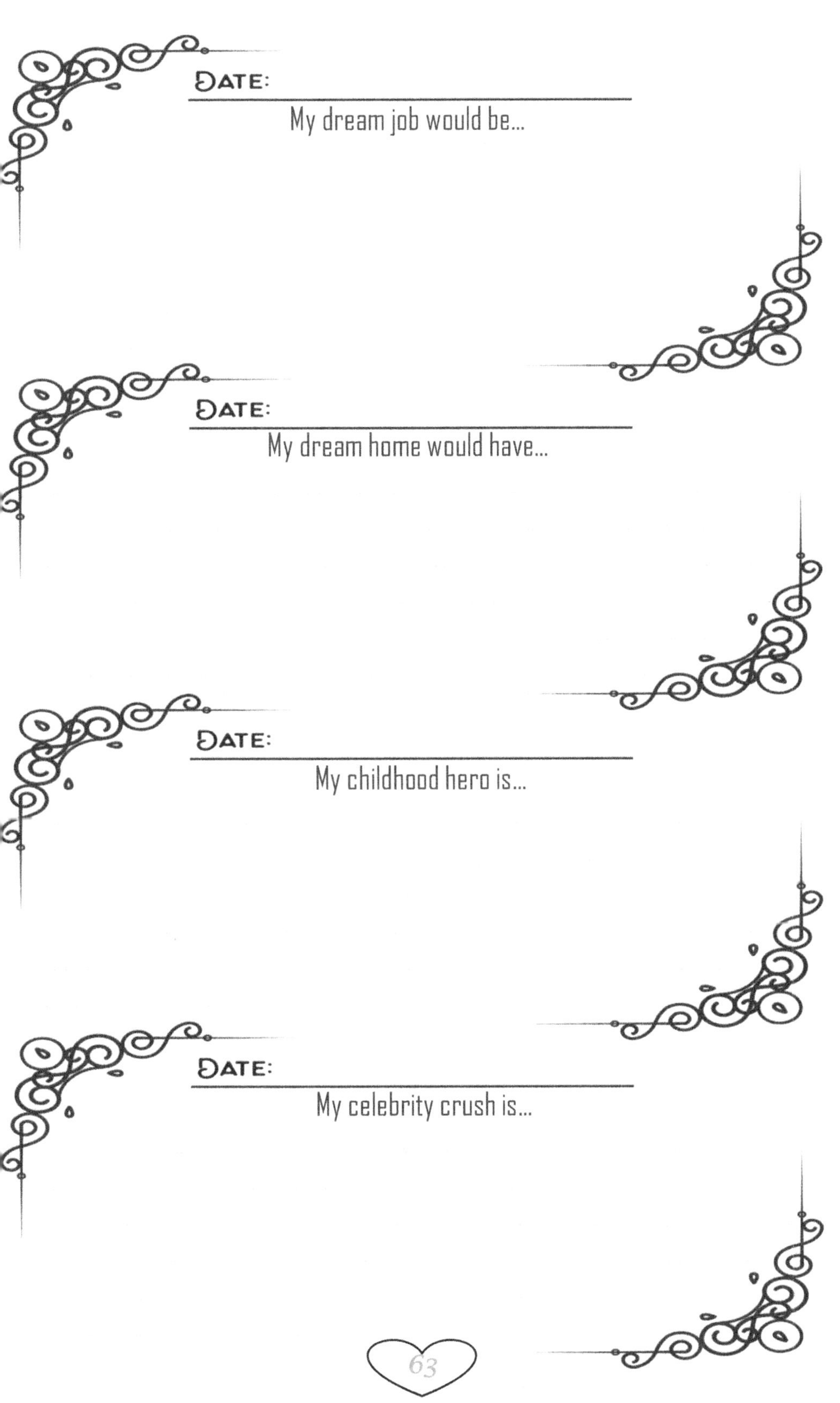

Date:

My dream job would be...

Date:

My dream home would have...

Date:

My childhood hero is...

Date:

My celebrity crush is...

Date:

My calm space looks like...

Date:

My biggest win this year was...

Date:

My biggest success was...

Date:

My biggest regret is...

DATE:

My biggest priority right now is...

DATE:

My biggest pet peeve is...

DATE:

My biggest nightmare is...

DATE:

My biggest challenge this year was...

Date:

My best year was...

Date:

My best talent is...

Date:

My best quality is...

Date:

My best friend would say I am...

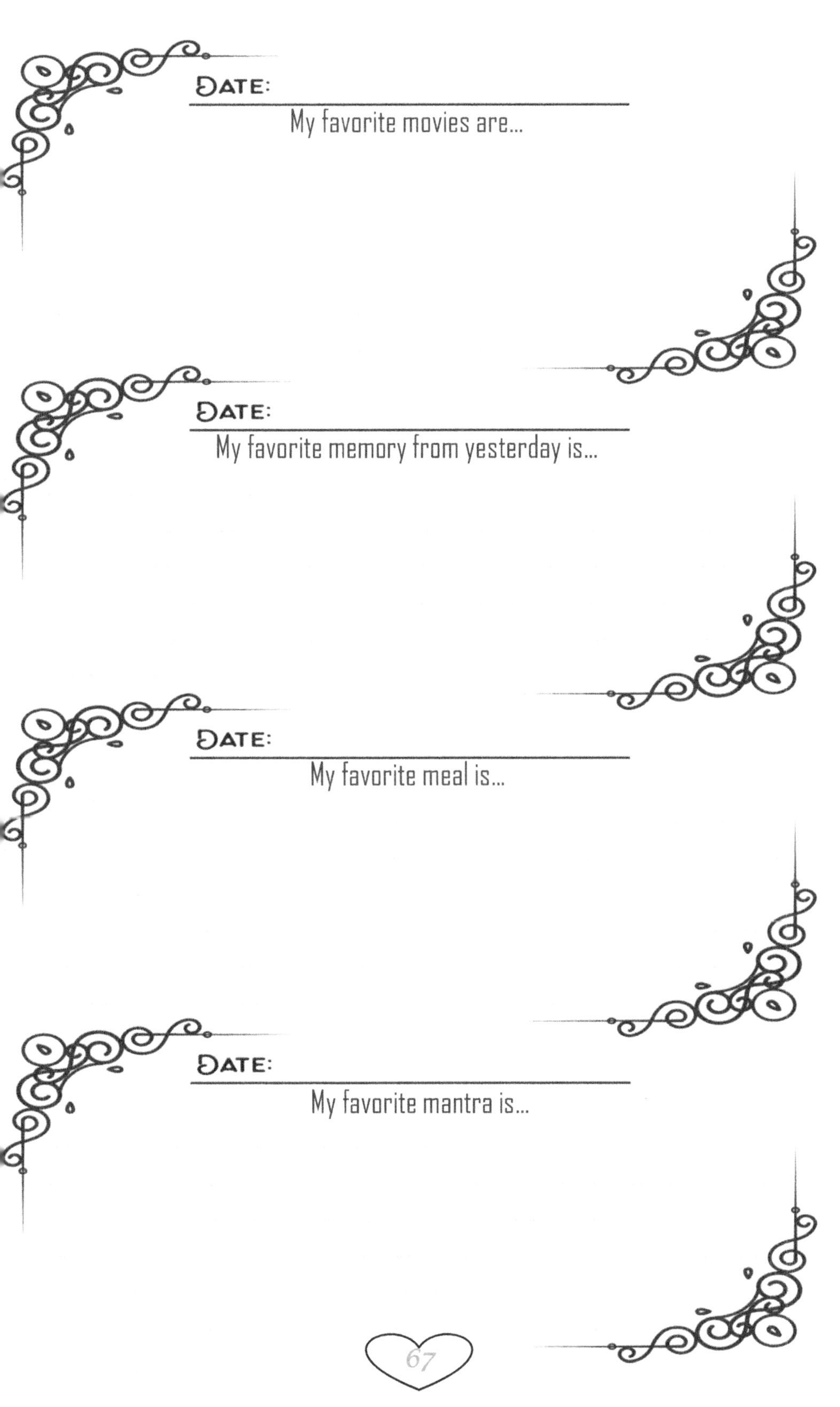

DATE:

My favorite movies are...

DATE:

My favorite memory from yesterday is...

DATE:

My favorite meal is...

DATE:

My favorite mantra is...

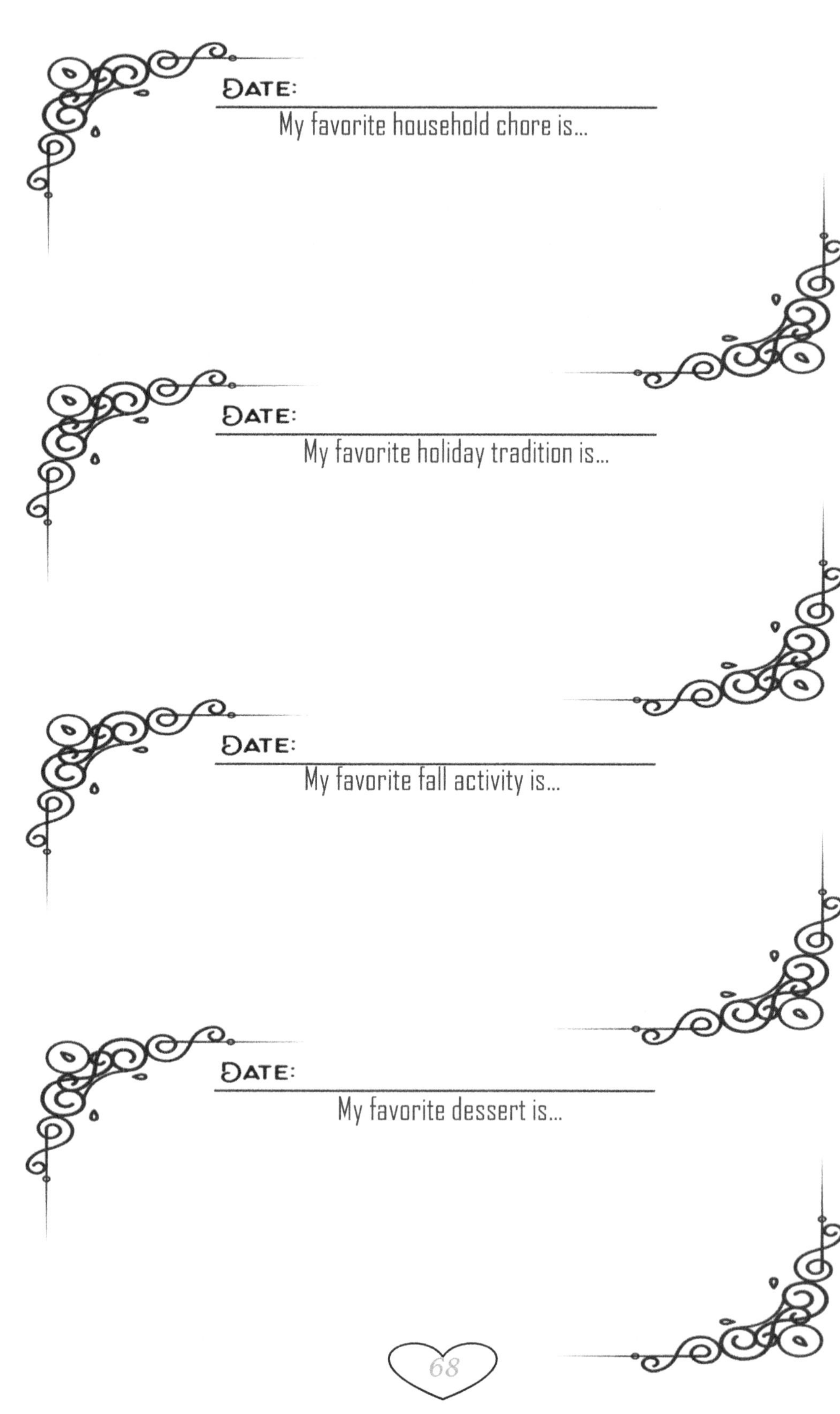

Date:

My favorite household chore is...

Date:

My favorite holiday tradition is...

Date:

My favorite fall activity is...

Date:

My favorite dessert is...

Pay Attention
TO THE CONSEQUENCES
Of Your Daily Habits

DATE:

My favorite daily ritual is...

DATE:

My favorite books are...

DATE:

My favorite book character is...

DATE:

My favorite body part is...

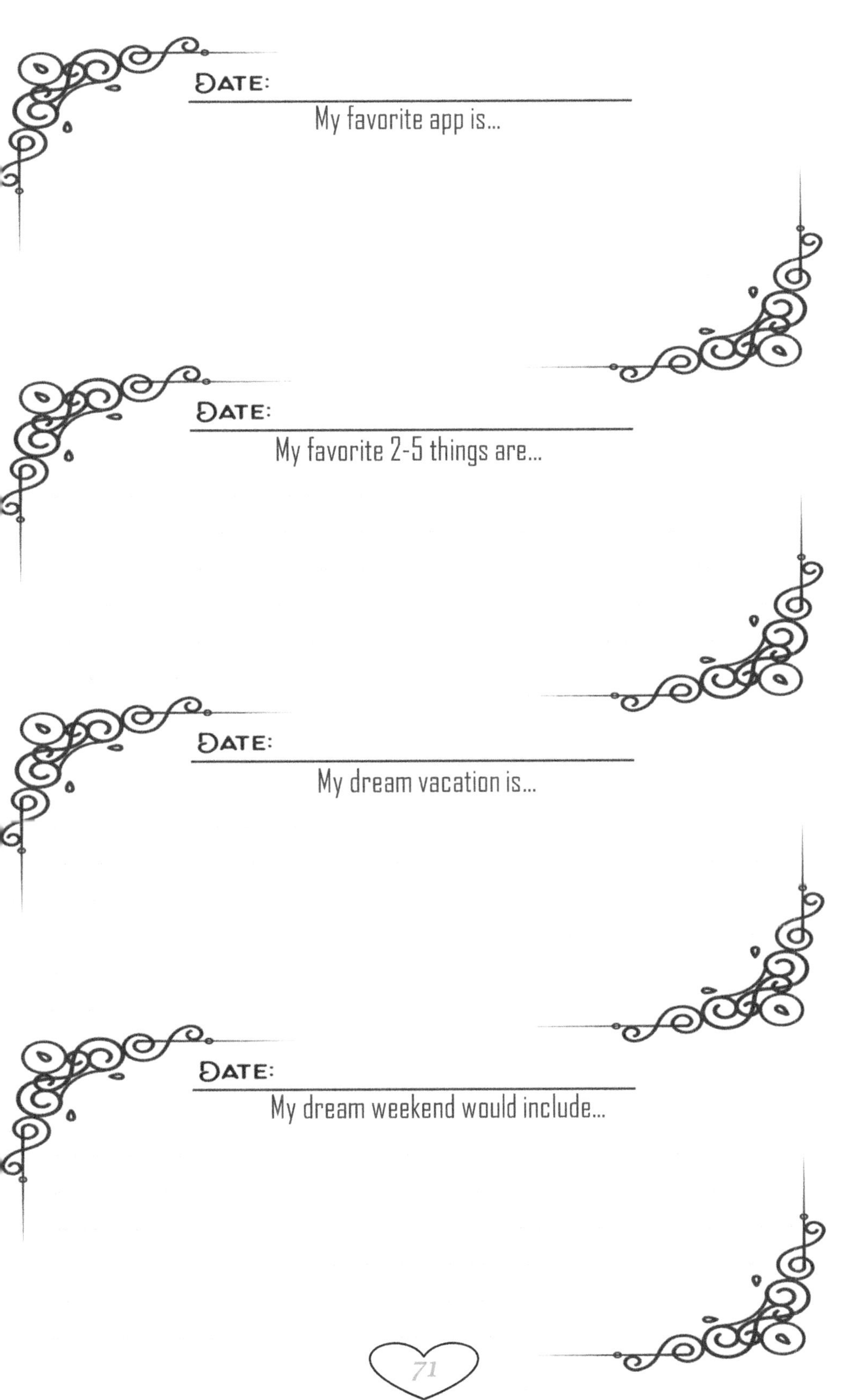

DATE:

My favorite app is...

DATE:

My favorite 2-5 things are...

DATE:

My dream vacation is...

DATE:

My dream weekend would include...

DATE:

My goals for today (this week, this year) are...

DATE:

My goals for next year are...

DATE:

My first memory is...

DATE:

My first job was...

Date:

My favorite winter activity is...

Date:

My favorite way to start the day is...

Date:

My favorite summer activity is...

Date:

My favorite spring activity is...

DATE:

My favorite song is...

DATE:

My favorite social gathering is...

DATE:

My favorite smell is...

DATE:

My favorite recipe is...

DATE:

My favorite quote is...

DATE:

My favorite place to visit is...

DATE:

My favorite part of nature is...

DATE:

My favorite part about my home is...

DATE:

My secret desire is...

DATE:

My relationship with my phone is...

DATE:

My perfect day would consist of...

DATE:

My philosophy of life is...

DATE:

My parents taught me...

DATE:

My next adventure will be...

DATE:

My most vivid childhood memory is...

DATE:

My most unrealistic worry is...

Never Let Others CONTROL YOUR MIND

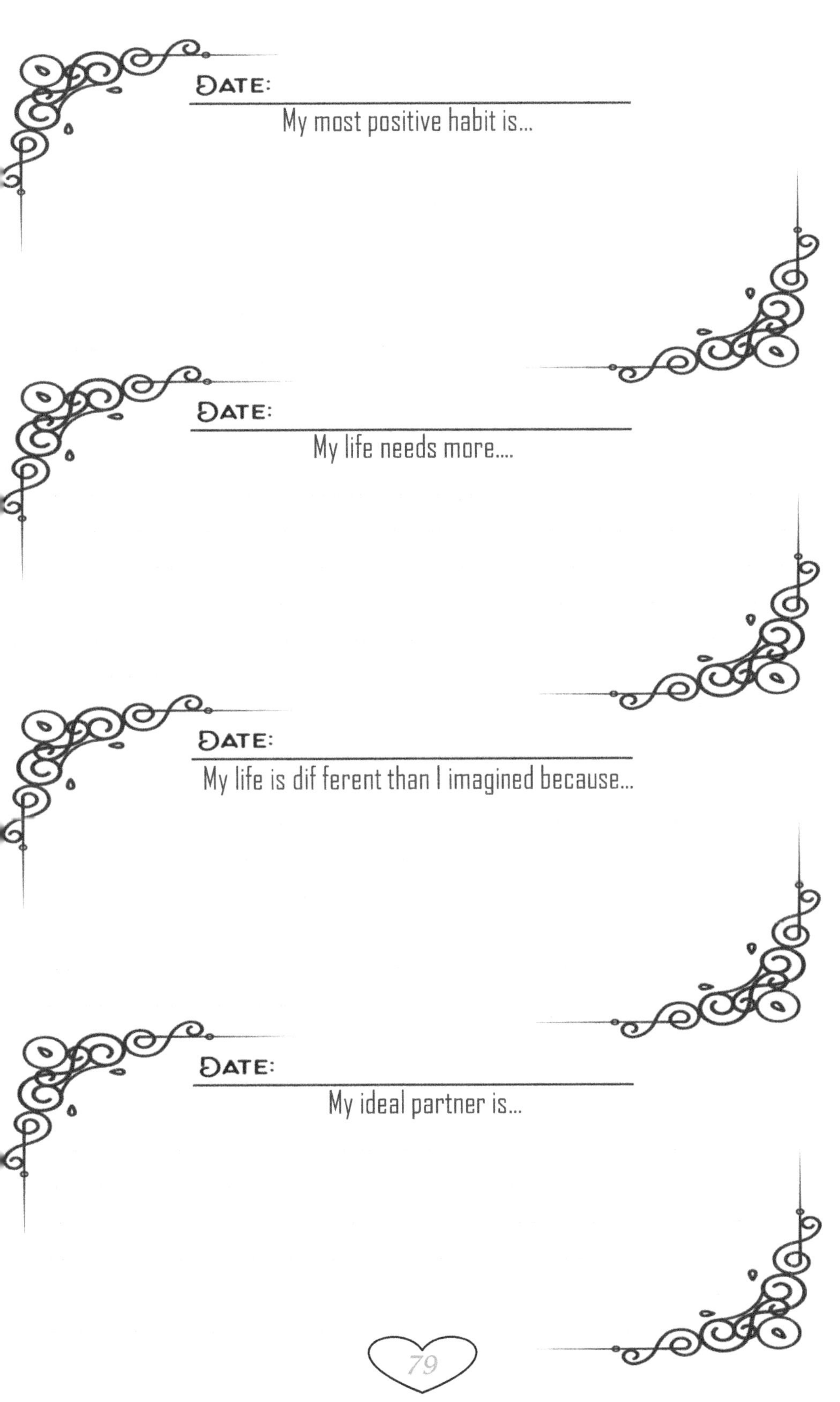

Date:

My most positive habit is...

Date:

My life needs more....

Date:

My life is dif ferent than I imagined because...

Date:

My ideal partner is...

Date:

My ideal nighttime routine would include...

Date:

My ideal morning routine would include...

Date:

My ideal day would look like...

Date:

My happy place is...

DATE:

My word for this month is...

DATE:

My vision for my life is...

DATE:

My vision board would include...

DATE:

My ultimate goal is...

DATE:

My top three priorities right now are...

DATE:

My three favorite people are ___ because...

DATE:

My style icon is...

DATE:

My strongest personality trait is...

DATE:

The biggest thing holding me back is...

DATE:

The biggest stressor in my life is...

DATE:

The biggest problem I've ever solved was...

DATE:

The biggest mistake I made this week was...

Date:

The biggest lie I have ever told was...

Date:

The biggest character f law I need to work on is...

Date:

The best thing I did this week was...

Date:

The best part about being with me is...

DATE:

The best gift I've ever received was...

DATE:

The best compliment I've ever received is...

DATE:

The best compliment I've ever given was...

DATE:

People annoy me when they...

DATE: ____________________

Other people see me as...

DATE: ____________________

One simple thing that makes me happy is...

DATE: ____________________

Nobody knows that I...

DATE: ____________________

Next year, I want to be more...

DATE:

The past experience I learned the most from is...

DATE:

The most stressful part of my day is...

DATE:

The most inspirational place I've ever been is...

DATE:

The most peaceful part of my day is...

DATE:

The most important life lesson I've learned is...

DATE:

The hardest part of my day was...

DATE:

The most important items on my to-do list today are...

DATE:

The most fun I've had was when...

DATE:

The hardest I have ever worked was when...

DATE:

The future scares me because...

DATE:

The future excites me because...

DATE:

The funniest thing to happen to me this week was...

When The Student IS READY, The Master APPEARS

Date:

The five biggest life lessons I've learned so far are...

Date:

The first time I felt independent was...

Date:

The favorite thing in my closet is...

Date:

The easiest part of my day was...

Date:

Today I will find time to...

Date:

Today I have been craving...

Date:

Today I can have more fun by...

Date:

To me, self-care means...

Date:

To make myself healthier, I could start...

Date:

This year, I am most grateful for...

Date:

This week, I had fun...

Date:

This time next year, I will be...

DATE:

_____ could help me reach my goals by...

DATE:

This isn't working in my life right now...

DATE:

These three features define me...

DATE:

These people make me feel the most loved...

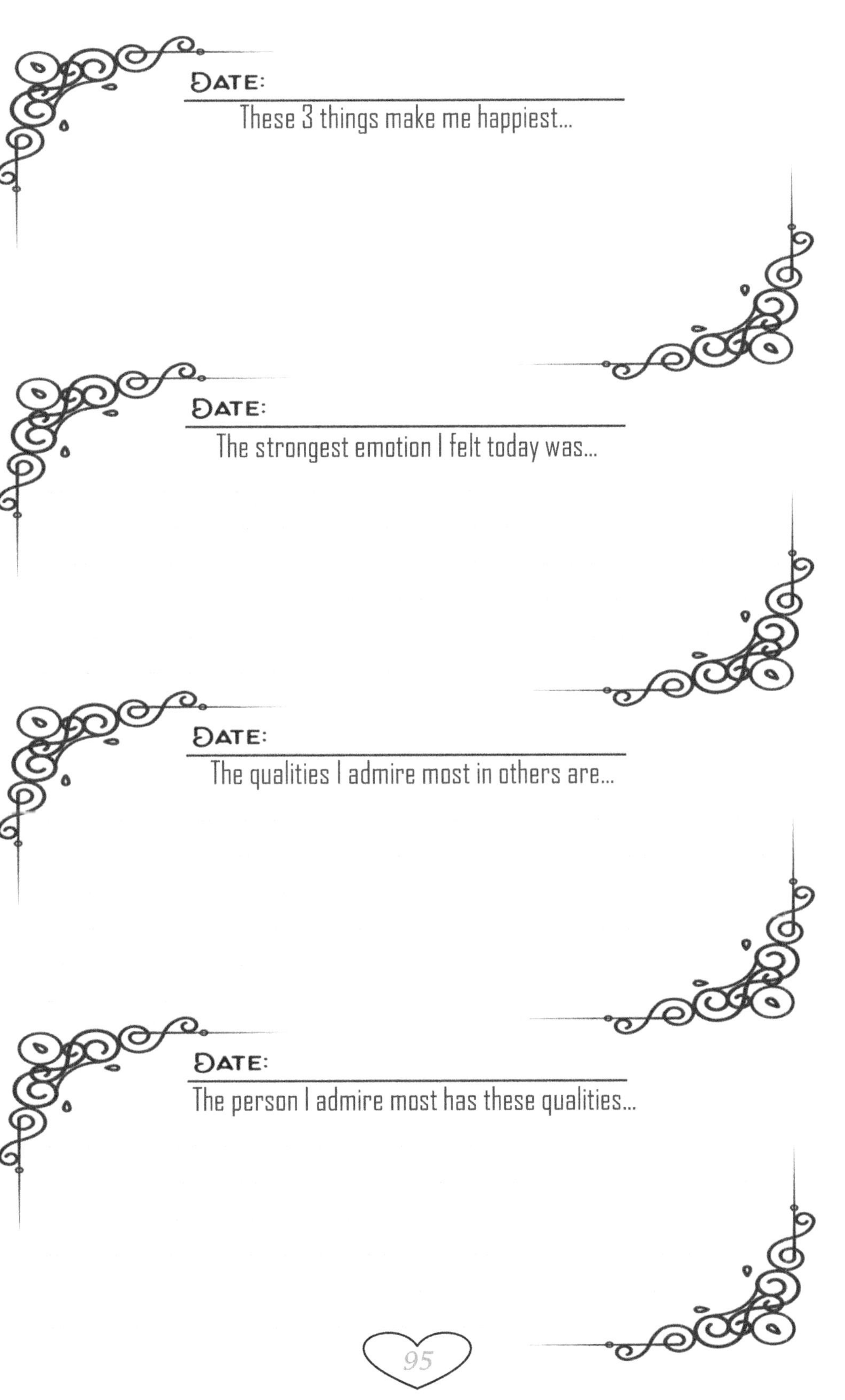

DATE:

These 3 things make me happiest...

DATE:

The strongest emotion I felt today was...

DATE:

The qualities I admire most in others are...

DATE:

The person I admire most has these qualities...

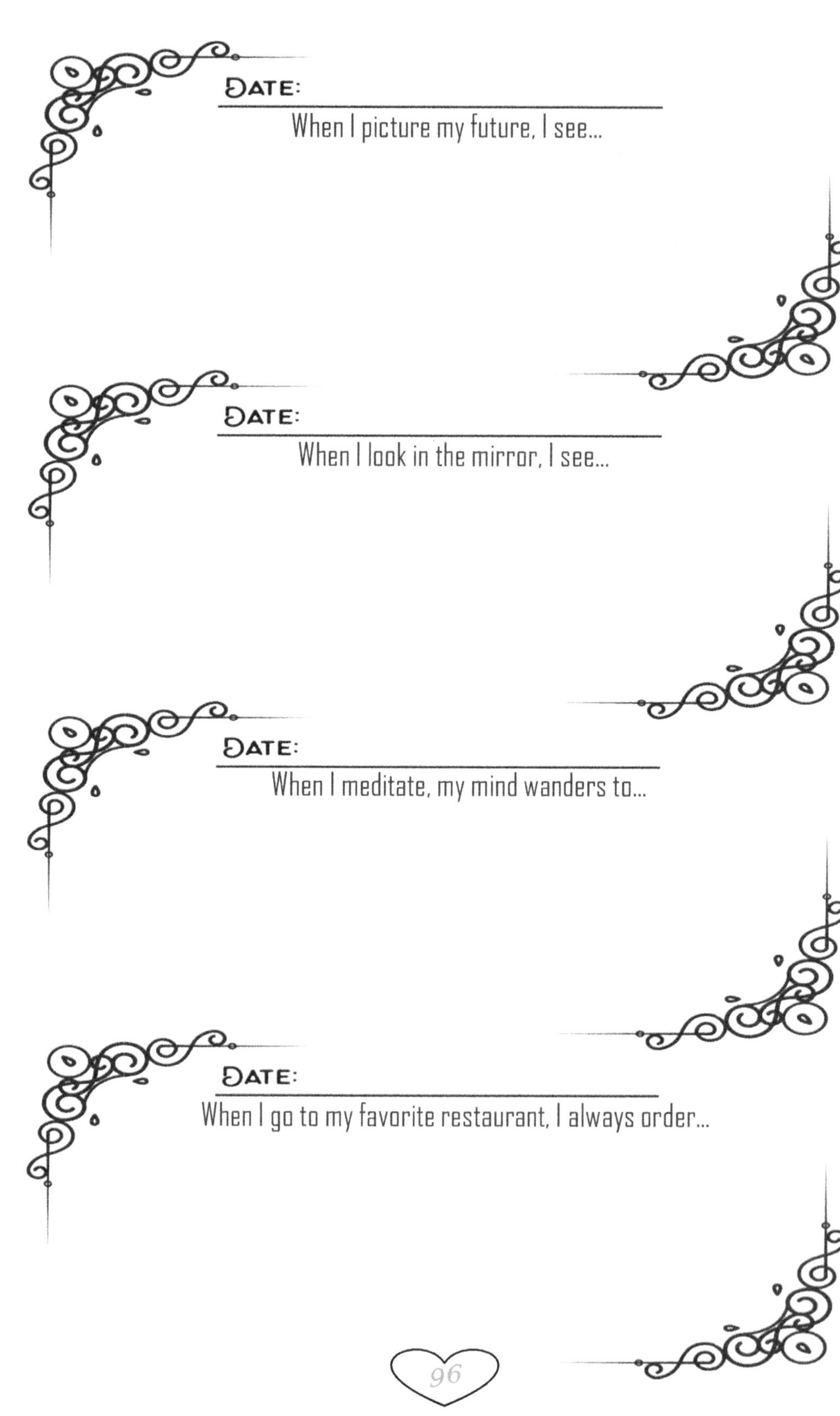

Date:

When I picture my future, I see...

Date:

When I look in the mirror, I see...

Date:

When I meditate, my mind wanders to...

Date:

When I go to my favorite restaurant, I always order...

Date:

When I feel confident, I can...

Date:

When I do _____, I feel strong because...

Date:

Tomorrow, I want to accomplish...

Date:

When I close my eyes at night, I think about...

DATE:

Today's plan is...

DATE:

Today's affirmation will be...

DATE:

Today, I will try something new by...

DATE:

Today, I will relax by...

DATE:

Today, I learned...

DATE:

Today, I can encourage someone to...

DATE:

Today was meaningful because...

DATE:

Today, I am grateful for...

DATE:

When others meet me for the first time, they probably think...

DATE:

When I was a child, I wanted...

DATE:

DATE:

Slow Progress

IS BETTER THAN NO PROGRESS.

Stay Positive AND Don't Give Up

Note

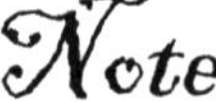

Note

Note

Note

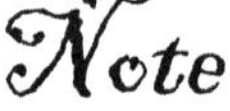

Note

Note

Note

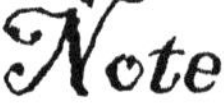

Made in the USA
Monee, IL
26 April 2022

95487138R00070